All Colour Recipes

All Colour Recipes

First published in Great Britain in 1999 by
Parragon
Queen Street House
4-5 Queen Street
Bath
BA1 1HE

ISBN: 0-7525-2921-8

Produced by Haldane Mason, London

Printed in Italy

Material in this book has previously appeared in
*What's Cooking? Pasta, What's Cooking? Italian,
What's Cooking? Vegetarian* and
What's Cooking? Barbecue

Note
Cup measurements in this book are for
American cups. Tablespoons are assumed to be
15 ml. Unless otherwise stated, milk is assumed
to be full fat, eggs are medium and
pepper is freshly ground black pepper.

Contents

Introduction

Many changes in eating habits have taken place in recent times and the modern diet has become much more varied as it incorporates new dietary and culinary trends. This book has brought together a collection of recipes which demonstrates these trends in a colourful and practical style.

Time is an important factor in deciding what to cook due to the pace of modern life; there is less time to spend in the kitchen and an increased demand for recipes which are simple and quick to prepare. This not only involves quick cooking and preparation methods, but also the use of versatile ingredients which can be used in a number of impromptu dishes. Pasta which takes only minutes to cook and can be combined with virtually any ingredient and sauce, plays an important role in this cookbook.

Health concerns have also prompted changes in diet as we are advised to reduce our fat and salt intake. While meat is still a valuable source of vitamins, we are turning increasingly towards lower-fat alternatives such as fish, poultry and vegetables. The rise in vegetarianism is as much due to a greater awareness of health issues as an ethical rejection of meat.

This book offers you a mouthwatering selection of dishes which caters for a wide variety of dietary and culinary tastes. Whatever the occasion, you are sure to find the perfect dish within these pages – soups, salads, casseroles, bakes, roasts, stir-fries, barbecues and desserts.

Pasta is a universal favourite – it is easy to cook, economical and versatile. Pasta means 'paste' or 'dough' in Italian, and many pasta dishes have their origins in Italy, where pasta has been produced since the 13th century. More types of fresh and dried pasta are coming on to the market to inspire new variations on tried and tested recipes. As well as green pasta made with spinach, and red pasta flavoured with tomato paste, more unusual colours are available: saffron pasta is an attractive orange-yellow, beetroot pasta is a vibrant pink, and pasta coloured with squid ink is a dramatic black.

You can also buy or make pasta flavoured with garlic or herbs. Pasta comes in all sorts of shapes and sizes too; lasagne, cannelloni, penne, fettucine, fusilli and macaroni are just a few. The enjoyment of pasta depends on it being cooked to perfection; instructions are given on page 11.

Italy is divided up into many distinct culinary regions, and this book takes recipes from many of them. The recipes for three of the most useful sauces in Italian cuisine are given on pages 10-11. In addition, this book concludes with several very Italian – and very wicked – desserts such as Ricotta Ice Cream and Tiramisu.

Barbecuing is one of the most enjoyable ways of entertaining family or friends. Too often, barbecues consist of only burgers and sausages, but it takes very little effort to provide a delicious range of meat, fish and vegetable dishes to suit every palate. Each barbecuing recipe in this book is especially designed to take full advantage of the succulent flavour that cooking over a barbecue gives. There are even some tempting barbecued dishes for vegetarians, such as Stuffed Red (Bell) Peppers and Filled Jacket Potatoes.

When shopping with a vegetarian meal in mind, make sure you are not buying animal products unawares. Choose cheese that is made from vegetarian rennet; buy agar-agar or gelozone instead of gelatine and select a vegetarian suet instead of beef suet. Stock your cupboard with a selection of staple ingredients like flours, grains, pastas and pulses. Nuts, seeds and dried fruits are a good source of proteins, vitamins and minerals. An essential base for many vegetarian dishes is a good stock, a recipe for which is given on page 192. Make a whole batch of stock at one go; it will keep for up to three days in the refrigerator, or for up to 3 months if frozen. Salt is not added when cooking the stock; it is better to season it according to the dish in which it is being used.

Whether you have decided to avoid meat and fish completely, or simply want a healthier diet, the section on vegetable dishes will show just how exciting vegetarian cookery has become. These recipes use fresh ingredients to produce meals that are good for your taste buds as well as your health.

This colourful cookbook contains delicious recipes which cater for a variety of tastes – there's sure to be something to tempt you!

Béchamel Sauce

300 ml / ½ pint / 1¼ cups milk • 2 bay leaves
3 cloves • 1 small onion
60 g / 2 oz / 4 tbsp butter • 40 g / 1½ oz / ⅓ cup flour
300 ml / ½ pint / 1¼ cups single (light) cream
large pinch of grated nutmeg
salt and pepper

1 Pour the milk into a small pan and add the bay leaves. Press the cloves into the onion, add to the pan and bring the milk to the boil. Remove the pan from the heat and set aside to cool.

2 Strain the milk into a jug and rinse the pan. Melt the butter in the pan, add the flour and stir for 1 minute. Gradually pour the milk into the pan, stirring constantly. Cook the sauce for 3 minutes, then add the cream and bring to the boil. Remove from the heat and season with nutmeg, salt and pepper.

Tomato Sauce

2 tbsp olive oil • 1 small onion, chopped
1 garlic clove, chopped
1 × 400 g / 14 oz can of chopped tomatoes
2 tbsp chopped parsley • 1 tsp dried oregano
2 bay leaves • 2 tbsp tomato purée (paste)
1 tsp sugar

1 Heat the oil in a pan over a medium heat and cook the onion until it is translucent. Add the garlic and cook for 1 minute.

2 Stir in the tomatoes, parsley, oregano, bay leaves, tomato purée (paste) and sugar and bring to the boil. Simmer, uncovered, for 15–20 minutes until the sauce has reduced by half. Taste and adjust the seasoning if necessary. Discard the bay leaves before serving.

Lamb Sauce

2 tbsp olive oil

1 large onion, sliced

2 celery stalks, thinly sliced

500 g/ 1 lb 2 oz lean lamb, minced (ground)

3 tbsp tomato purée (paste)

150 g/ 5½ oz bottled sun-dried tomatoes, drained and chopped

1 tsp dried oregano

1 tbsp red wine vinegar

150 ml/ ¼ pint/ ⅔ cups chicken stock

salt and pepper

1 Heat the oil in a frying pan (skillet) over a medium heat. Add the onion and celery and cook until the onion is translucent. Add the lamb and cook, stirring frequently, until it browns.

2 Stir in the tomato purée (paste), sun-dried tomatoes, oregano, red wine vinegar and chicken stock, and season with salt and pepper to taste.

3 Bring the sauce to the boil and cook, uncovered, for about 20 minutes until the meat has absorbed the stock. Taste the sauce and adjust the seasoning if necessary.

Cooking Pasta

Cook pasta in a large pan of salted boiling water, to which you have added 1 tablespoon of olive oil; this will prevent the pieces of pasta from sticking together. When the pasta is almost tender, with a slight bite to it – the Italians describe it as *al dente* – remove from the heat and drain well in a colander.

Cooking times vary according to the type and volume of the pasta, and you should always follow those recommended on the packet. In general, fresh pasta cooks in 3–5 minutes, while dried pasta takes around 6 minutes.

Soups & Starters

The soup recipes in this chapter are ideal appetizers, but served with chunks of crusty bread will make a satisfying meal in their own right. The starters featured here are so versatile that not only are they tempting appetizers, but they could also be used to liven up a picnic or buffet.

Spinach & Mascarpone Soup

This delicious soup has Mascarpone cheese stirred through it to give it the most wonderful texture and flavour.

SERVES 4

60 g / 2 oz / 4 tbsp butter
1 bunch spring onions (scallions), trimmed and chopped
2 celery sticks, chopped
350 g / 12 oz / 3 cups spinach or sorrel, or 3 bunches watercress
900 ml / 1½ pints / 3½ cups vegetable stock
250 g / 8 oz Mascarpone cheese • 1 tbsp olive oil
2 slices thick-cut bread, cut into cubes
½ tsp caraway seeds • salt and pepper
sesame bread sticks, to serve

1 Melt half the butter in a very large saucepan. Add the spring onions (scallions) and celery, and cook gently for about 5 minutes, until softened. Pack the spinach, sorrel or watercress into the saucepan. Add the stock and bring to the boil; then reduce the heat and simmer, covered, for 15–20 minutes.

2 Transfer the soup to a blender or food processor and blend until smooth, or rub through a sieve. Return the soup to the saucepan. Add the Mascarpone cheese and heat gently, stirring, until smooth and blended. Season to taste.

3 Heat the remaining butter with the oil in a frying pan (skillet). Add the bread cubes and fry in the hot fat until golden brown, adding the caraway seeds towards the end of cooking, so that they do not burn.

4 Ladle the soup into 4 warmed bowls. Sprinkle with the croûtons and serve at once, accompanied by the sesame bread sticks.

Hot & Sour Soup

A traditional staple of the Thai diet, this delicious and nourishing vegetarian soup is sold on street corners, at food bars and by mobile vendors all over the country.

SERVES 4

1 tbsp sunflower oil
250 g/ 8 oz smoked tofu (bean curd), sliced
90 g/ 3 oz/ 1 cup shiitake mushrooms, sliced
2 tbsp chopped fresh coriander (cilantro)
125 g/ 4 oz/ 2 cups watercress
1 red chilli, sliced finely, to garnish

Stock:

1 tbsp tamarind pulp
2 dried red chillies, chopped
2 kaffir lime leaves, torn in half
2.5 cm/ 1 inch piece ginger root, chopped
5 cm/ 2 inch piece galangal, chopped
1 stalk lemon grass, chopped
1 onion, quartered
1 litre/ 1¾ pints/ 4 cups cold water

1 Put all the ingredients for the stock into a saucepan and bring to the boil. Simmer for 5 minutes. Remove from the heat and strain, reserving the stock.

2 Heat the oil in a wok or large, heavy frying pan (skillet) and cook the tofu (bean curd) over a high heat for about 2 minutes, stirring constantly. Pour in the strained stock.

3 Add the mushrooms and coriander (cilantro), and boil for 3 minutes.

4 Add the watercress and boil for 1 minute more. Serve at once, garnished with chilli slices.

Fish Soup

The selection of Italian fish soups is enormous. This one, from Tuscany, is more like a chowder.

SERVES 4–6

1 kg/2 lb assorted prepared fish (including mixed fish fillets, squid, etc.)
2 onions, thinly sliced • a few sprigs of parsley
2 bay leaves • 2 celery sticks, thinly sliced
150 ml/¼ pint/⅔ cup white wine
1 litre/1¾ pints/4 cups water
2 tbsp olive oil • 1 garlic clove, crushed
1 carrot, peeled and finely chopped
425 g/14 oz can of peeled tomatoes, puréed
2 potatoes, peeled and chopped • 1 tbsp tomato purée (paste)
1 tsp freshly chopped oregano or ½ tsp dried oregano
350 g/12 oz fresh mussels
175 g/6 oz peeled prawns (shrimp)
2 tbsp freshly chopped parsley • salt and pepper
crusty bread, to serve

1 Cut the cleaned and prepared fish into slices or cubes and put into a large saucepan with 1 sliced onion, the parsley sprigs and bay leaves, 1 sliced celery stick, the wine and the water. Bring to the boil, cover and simmer for about 25 minutes.

2 Strain the fish stock and discard the vegetables. Skin the fish, remove any bones and reserve.

3 Heat the oil in a pan, finely chop the remaining onion and fry with the garlic, remaining celery and carrot until soft but not coloured. Add the puréed canned tomatoes, potatoes, tomato purée (paste), oregano, reserved stock and seasonings. Bring to the boil and simmer for about 15 minutes or until the potato is almost tender.

4 Meanwhile, thoroughly scrub the mussels. Add to the pan with the prawns (shrimp) and simmer for about 5 minutes or until the mussels have opened (discard any that remain closed).

5 Return the fish to the soup and add the chopped parsley, bring back to the boil and simmer for 5 minutes. Adjust the seasoning, if necessary.

6 Serve the soup in warmed bowls with chunks of fresh crusty bread, or put a toasted slice of crusty bread in the bottom of each bowl before adding the soup. If possible, remove a few half shells from the mussels before serving.

Minestrone with Pesto

Minestrone always contains a variety of vegetables, pasta and rice. This version also includes beans.

SERVES 6

175 g/ 6 oz/ scant 1 cup dried cannellini beans, soaked overnight
2½ litres/ 4 pints/ 10 cups water or stock
1 large onion, chopped • 1 leek, trimmed and sliced thinly
2 celery stalks, sliced very thinly • 2 carrots, chopped
3 tbsp olive oil • 2 tomatoes, peeled and chopped roughly
1 courgette (zucchini), trimmed and sliced thinly
2 potatoes, diced
90 g/ 3 oz elbow macaroni, or other small macaroni
salt and pepper • 4–6 tbsp freshly grated Parmesan

Pesto:
2 tbsp pine kernels (nuts) • 5 tbsp olive oil
2 bunches basil, stems removed
4–6 garlic cloves, crushed
90 g/ 3 oz/ 1 cup Pecorino or Parmesan, grated
salt and pepper

1 Drain the beans, rinse and put in a saucepan with the water or stock. Bring to the boil, cover and simmer gently for 1 hour. Add the onion, leek, celery, carrots and oil to the pan. Cover and simmer for 4–5 minutes. Add the tomatoes, courgette (zucchini), potatoes and macaroni and season. Cover again and continue to simmer for about 30 minutes or until very tender.

2 Meanwhile, make the pesto. Fry the pine kernels (nuts) in 1 tablespoon of the oil until pale brown, then drain. Put the basil into a food processor or blender with the nuts and garlic. Process until well chopped. Alternatively, chop finely by

hand and pound with a
pestle and mortar. Gradually
add the oil until smooth.
Turn into a bowl, add the
cheese and season to taste,
and mix thoroughly.

3 Stir 1 1/2 tablespoons of
the pesto into the soup
until well blended. Simmer
for a further 5 minutes and
adjust the seasoning, if
necessary. Serve very hot,
sprinkled with the cheese.

Herb, Toasted Nut & Paprika Cheese Nibbles

These tiny cheese balls are rolled in fresh herbs, toasted nuts or paprika to make tasty nibbles for parties, buffets, or pre-dinner drinks.

SERVES 4

125 g/ 4 oz/ ³⁄₄ cup Ricotta
125 g/ 4 oz/ 1¼ cups Double Gloucester (brick) cheese, grated
2 tsp chopped parsley • pepper
60 g/ 2 oz/ ½ cup chopped mixed nuts
3 tbsp chopped fresh herbs, such as parsley, chives, marjoram, lovage and chervil
2 tbsp mild paprika
sprigs of fresh herbs, to garnish

1 Mix together the Ricotta and Double Gloucester (brick) cheeses. Add the parsley and pepper, and mix together until combined.

2 Form the mixture into small balls. Cover and chill for about 20 minutes to firm.

3 Scatter the chopped nuts on to a baking sheet (cookie sheet) and place them under a preheated grill (broiler) until lightly browned. Take care as they can easily burn. Leave them to cool.

4 Sprinkle the nuts, herbs and paprika into 3 separate small bowls. Divide the cheese balls into 3 equal piles and then roll 1 quantity in the nuts, 1 quantity in the herbs and 1 quantity in the paprika.

5 Arrange on a serving platter. Chill until ready to serve, and then garnish with sprigs of fresh herbs.

Cheese, Garlic & Herb Pâté

This wonderfully soft cheese pâté is fragrant with the aroma of fresh herbs.

SERVES 4

15 g/½ oz/1 tbsp butter • 1 garlic clove, crushed
3 spring onions (scallions), chopped finely
125 g/4 oz/¾ cup full-fat soft cheese
2 tbsp chopped mixed fresh herbs, such as parsley, chives,
marjoram, oregano and basil
175 g/6 oz/2¼ cups mature (sharp) Cheddar, grated
pepper
4–6 slices of white bread from a medium-cut sliced loaf
mixed salad leaves (greens) and cherry tomatoes, to serve

To garnish:
ground paprika • sprigs of fresh herbs

1 Melt the butter in a small frying pan (skillet) and gently fry the garlic and spring onions (scallions) for 3–4 minutes, until softened. Allow to cool.

2 Beat the soft cheese in a large mixing bowl, then add the garlic and spring onions (scallions). Stir in the herbs, mixing well. Add the Cheddar and work the mixture together to form a stiff paste. Cover and chill until ready to serve.

3 Toast the slices of bread on both sides, then cut off the crusts. Using a sharp bread knife, cut through the slices horizontally to make very thin slices. Cut into triangles and then lightly grill (broil) the untoasted sides.

4 Arrange the mixed salad leaves (green) on 4 serving plates with the tomatoes. Pile the pâté on top and sprinkle with a little paprika. Garnish with fresh herbs and serve with the Melba toast.

Heavenly Garlic Dip
with Crudités

**Anyone who loves garlic will adore this dip.
Keep it warm to one side of the barbecue,
and dip raw vegetables or hunks of
French bread into it.**

SERVES 4

*2 bulbs garlic, chopped finely • 6 tbsp olive oil
1 small onion, chopped finely
2 tbsp lemon juice
3 tbsp tahini (sesame seed paste)
2 tbsp chopped fresh parsley
salt and pepper*

To serve:
*fresh vegetable crudités
French bread or warmed pitta (pocket) breads*

1 Separate the bulbs of garlic into cloves. Place them on a baking (cookie) sheet and roast in a preheated oven at 200°C/400°F/Gas Mark 6 for 8–10 minutes. Leave to cool for a few minutes. Peel the garlic cloves, then chop them finely.

2 Heat the olive oil in a saucepan or frying pan (skillet) and add the garlic and onion. Fry for 8–10 minutes until softened. Remove the pan from the heat.

3 Mix the lemon juice, tahini (sesame seed paste) and parsley into the garlic mixture. Season to taste with salt and pepper. Transfer to a small heatproof bowl and keep warm at one side of the barbecue.

4 Serve with a selection of fresh vegetable crudités, chunks of French bread or warm pitta (pocket) breads.

Tzatziki with Pitta (Pocket) Breads & Black Olive Dip

Tzatziki is a Greek dish, made with natural yogurt, mint and cucumber.

SERVES 4

½ cucumber
250 g/8 oz/1 cup thick natural yogurt
1 tbsp chopped fresh mint
salt and pepper • 4 pitta (pocket) breads

Black olive dip:
2 garlic cloves, crushed
125 g/4 oz/¾ cup pitted black olives
4 tbsp olive oil • 2 tbsp lemon juice
1 tbsp chopped fresh parsley

To garnish:
sprigs of fresh mint • sprigs of fresh parsley

1 To make the tzatziki, peel the cucumber and chop roughly. Sprinkle with salt and leave to stand for 15–20 minutes. Rinse with cold water and drain well. Mix the cucumber, yogurt and mint together. Season with salt and pepper and transfer to a serving bowl. Cover and leave to chill for 20–30 minutes.

2 To make the dip, put the crushed garlic and olives into a blender or food processor and blend for 15–20 seconds. Add the olive oil, lemon juice and parsley and blend for a few seconds. Alternatively, chop the garlic and olives very finely. Mix the olive oil, lemon juice and parsley with the garlic and olives and mash together. Season with salt and pepper.

3 Wrap the pitta (pocket) breads in foil and place over the barbecue for 2–3

minutes, turning once to warm through. Alternatively, heat in the oven or under the grill (broiler). Cut the bread into pieces and serve with the tzatziki and black olive dip, garnished with sprigs of fresh mint and parsley.

Fiery Salsa with Tortilla Chips

Make this Mexican-style salsa to perk up jaded palates. Its lively flavours really get the tastebuds going.

SERVES 6

2 small red chillies
1 tbsp lime or lemon juice
2 large ripe avocados
5 cm/2 inch piece cucumber
2 tomatoes, peeled
1 small garlic clove, crushed
few drops of Tabasco sauce • salt and pepper
lime or lemon slices, to garnish
tortilla chips, to serve

1 Remove and discard the stem and seeds from 1 chilli. Chop very finely and place in a mixing bowl. To make a chilli 'flower' for garnish, slice the remaining chilli from the stem to the tip several times without removing the stem. Place in a bowl of cold water, so that the 'petals' open out.

2 Add the lime or lemon juice to the mixing bowl. Halve, stone (pit) and peel the avocados. Add to the mixing bowl and mash with a fork. (The lime or lemon juice prevents the avocado from turning brown.)

3 Chop the cucumber and tomatoes finely and add to the avocado mixture with the crushed garlic. Season the dip to taste with Tabasco sauce, salt and pepper.

4 Transfer the dip to a serving bowl. Garnish with slices of lime or lemon and the chilli flower. Put the bowl on a large plate, surround with tortilla chips and serve.

Mint & Bean Dip

This dip is ideal for pre-dinner drinks or handing around at a party, accompanied by crisps and colourful vegetable crudités.

SERVES 6

175 g/6 oz/1 cup dried cannellini beans
1 small garlic clove, crushed
1 bunch spring onions (scallions), chopped roughly
handful of fresh mint leaves
2 tbsp tahini (sesame seed paste) • 2 tbsp olive oil
1 tsp ground cumin
1 tsp ground coriander • lemon juice
salt and pepper • sprigs of fresh mint, to garnish

To serve:
fresh vegetable crudités, such as cauliflower florets, carrots, cucumber, radishes and (bell) peppers

1 Soak the cannellini beans overnight in plenty of cold water.

2 Rinse and drain the beans, put them into a large saucepan and cover them with cold water. Bring to the boil and boil rapidly for 10 minutes. Reduce the heat, cover and simmer until tender.

3 Drain the beans and transfer them to a bowl or food processor. Add the garlic, spring onions (scallions), mint, tahini and olive oil.

4 Blend the mixture for about 15 seconds, or mash well by hand, until smooth.

5 Transfer the mixture to a bowl and season with cumin, coriander, lemon juice, salt and pepper, according to taste. Mix well, cover and leave in a cool place for 30 minutes to allow the flavours to develop.

6 Spoon the dip into serving bowls, garnish with sprigs of fresh mint and surround with vegetable crudités.

Baked Aubergine (Eggplant), Basil & Mozzarella Rolls

Thin slices of aubergine (eggplant) are fried in olive oil and garlic, then topped with pesto sauce and Mozzarella.

SERVES 4

2 aubergines (eggplant), sliced thinly lengthways
5 tbsp olive oil • 1 garlic clove, crushed
4 tbsp pesto sauce
175 g / 6 oz / 2¼ cups Mozzarella, grated
basil leaves, torn into pieces
salt and pepper
fresh basil leaves, to garnish

1 Sprinkle the aubergine (eggplant) slices liberally with salt and leave for 10–15 minutes to extract the bitter juices. Turn the slices over and repeat. Rinse well with cold water and drain on paper towels.

2 Heat the olive oil in a large frying pan (skillet) and add the garlic. Fry the aubergine (eggplant) slices lightly on both sides, a few at a time. Drain them on paper towels.

3 Spread the pesto on to one side of the aubergine (eggplant) slices. Top with the grated Mozzarella and sprinkle with the torn basil leaves. Season with a little salt and pepper. Roll up the slices and secure with wooden cocktail sticks (toothpicks).

4 Arrange the aubergine (eggplant) rolls in a greased ovenproof baking dish. Place in a preheated oven, 180°C/350°F/Gas Mark 4, and bake for 8–10 minutes.

5 Transfer the rolls to a warmed serving plate. Scatter with fresh basil leaves and serve at once.

Mozzarella in Carozza

**A delicious way of serving Mozzarella –
the cheese stretches out into melted strings
as you cut into the Carozza.**

SERVES 4

*200 g/7 oz Mozzarella
4 slices, Parma ham (prosciutto), about 90 g/3 oz
8 two-day-old slices of white bread, crusts removed
butter for spreading • 2–3 eggs
3 tbsp milk • vegetable oil for deep-frying
salt and pepper*

Tomato & pepper sauce:

*1 onion, chopped • 2 garlic cloves, crushed
3 tbsp olive oil
1 red (bell) pepper, cored, deseeded and chopped
400 g/14 oz can of peeled tomatoes
2 tbsp tomato purée (paste) • 3 tbsp water
1 tbsp lemon juice • salt and pepper
flat-leaf parsley, to garnish (optional)*

1 First make the sauce: fry the onion and garlic in the oil until soft. Add the (bell) pepper and continue to cook for 2–3 minutes. Add the tomatoes, tomato purée (paste), water, lemon juice and seasoning. Bring to the boil, cover and simmer for 10–15 minutes or until tender. Cool the sauce a little, then purée or liquidize until smooth and return to a clean pan.

2 Cut the Mozzarella into 4 slices as large as possible; if using a square piece of cheese, cut into 8 slices. Trim the Parma ham (prosciutto) slices to the same size as the cheese. Lightly butter the bread and use the cheese and ham to make 4 sandwiches, pressing the edges together firmly. If liked, they may be cut in half at this stage. Cover with cling film (plastic wrap) and chill.

3 Lightly beat the eggs with the milk and seasoning in a shallow dish. Carefully dip the sandwiches in the egg mixture until well coated, and leave to soak for a few minutes, if possible.

4 Heat the oil in a large pan or deep-frier to 180°C–190°C/350°C–375°F,

or until a cube of bread browns in about 30 seconds. Fry the sandwiches in batches until golden brown on both sides. Drain well on paper towels and keep warm.

5 Serve the sandwiches hot, with the reheated tomato and pepper sauce, garnished with parsley, if using.

Crostini alla Fiorentina

Serve as a starter, or simply spread on small pieces of crusty fried bread (crostini) as an appetizer with drinks.

SERVES 4

3 tbsp olive oil • 1 onion, chopped
1 celery stalk, chopped • 1 carrot, chopped
1–2 garlic cloves, crushed • 125 g/4 oz chicken livers
125 g/4 oz calf's, lamb's or pig's liver
150 ml/¼ pint/⅔ cup red wine
1 tbsp tomato purée (paste)
2 tbsp chopped fresh parsley
3–4 canned anchovy fillets, chopped finely
2 tbsp stock or water
30–45 g/1–1½ oz/2–3 tbsp butter • 1 tbsp capers
salt and pepper • small pieces of fried crusty bread, to serve
chopped parsley, to garnish

1 Heat the oil in a pan, add the onion, celery, carrot and garlic, and cook gently for 4–5 minutes or until the onion is soft, but not coloured.

2 Meanwhile, rinse and dry the chicken livers. Dry the calf's, lamb's or pig's liver, and slice into strips. Add the liver to the pan and fry gently for a few minutes until the strips are well sealed on all sides.

3 Add half the wine and cook until mostly evaporated. Then add the rest of the wine, tomato purée (paste), half the parsley, the anchovy fillets, stock or water, a little salt and plenty of black pepper. Cover the pan and simmer for 15–20 minutes or until tender and most of the liquid has been absorbed. Let the mixture cool a little, then either coarsely mince or put into a food processor and process to a chunky purée.

4 Return to the pan and add the butter, capers

and remaining parsley. Heat
through gently until the
butter melts. Adjust the
seasoning and turn into a
bowl. Serve warm or cold,
spread on the slices of crusty
bread and sprinkled with
chopped parsley.

Salads & Light Meals

With so many fresh ingredients available, it is easy to create some deliciously different and inventive salads, as you will see from this chapter. The recipes for light meals offer something for every taste – vegetables, cheese and meat, together with a variety of pasta shapes.

Mango Salad

This popular Thai salad is an unusual combination of ingredients, but works well as long as the mango is very unripe. Paw-paw (papaya) can be used instead, if you prefer. The components of the salad can be prepared ahead, but should not be assembled until just before serving, so that the flavours remain distinct.

SERVES 4

1 lollo blondo lettuce, or any crunchy lettuce
15 g / ½ oz fresh coriander (cilantro) leaves
1 large unripe mango, peeled and
cut into long thin shreds
1 small red chilli, deseeded and chopped finely
2 shallots, chopped finely
2 tbsp lemon juice
1 tbsp light soy sauce
6 roasted canned chestnuts, quartered

1 Line a serving plate or watermelon basket with the lettuce and coriander (cilantro).

2 Soak the mango briefly in cold water, in order to remove any syrup.

3 Meanwhile, make the dressing. Combine the chilli, shallots, lemon juice and soy sauce in a small bowl.

4 Drain the mango, combine with the chestnuts and spoon on to the lettuce and coriander (cilantro).

5 Pour over the dressing and serve immediately.

Pink Grapefruit, Avocado & Dolcelatte Salad

**Fresh pink grapefruit segments,
ripe avocados and sliced Italian Dolcelatte
cheese make a deliciously different
salad combination.**

SERVES 4

½ cos (romaine) lettuce
½ oak leaf lettuce
2 pink grapefruit • 2 ripe avocados
175 g/ 6 oz Dolcelatte cheese, sliced thinly
sprigs of fresh basil to garnish

Dressing:
4 tbsp olive oil • 1 tbsp white wine vinegar
salt and pepper

1 Arrange the lettuce leaves on 4 serving plates or in a salad bowl.

2 Remove the peel and pith from the grapefruit with a sharp serrated knife, catching the grapefruit juice in a bowl.

3 Segment the grapefruit by cutting down each side of the membrane. Remove all the membrane. Arrange the segments on the serving plates.

4 Peel, stone (pit) and slice the avocados, dipping them in the grapefruit juice to prevent them from going brown. Arrange the slices on the salad with the Dolcelatte cheese.

5 To make the dressing, combine any remaining grapefruit juice with the olive oil and wine vinegar. Season with salt and pepper, mixing well.

6 Drizzle the dressing over the salads. Garnish with fresh basil leaves and serve at once.

Red Onion, Cherry Tomato & Pasta Salad

Pasta tastes perfect in this lively salad.

SERVES 4

175 g/ 6 oz pasta shapes
1 yellow (bell) pepper, halved, cored and deseeded
2 small courgettes (zucchini), sliced
1 red onion, sliced thinly
125 g/ 4 oz cherry tomatoes, halved
salt • sprigs of fresh basil, to garnish

Dressing:

4 tbsp olive oil • 2 tbsp red wine vinegar
2 tsp lemon juice • 1 tsp Dijon mustard
½ tsp caster (superfine) sugar • salt and pepper
handful of fresh basil leaves, torn into small pieces

1 Cook the pasta in a saucepan of boiling, salted water for about 8 minutes, or until just tender.

2 Meanwhile, place the (bell) pepper halves, skin-side uppermost, under a preheated grill (broiler) until they just begin to char. Leave them to cool, then peel and slice into strips.

3 Cook the courgettes (zucchini) in a small amount of boiling, lightly salted water for 3–4 minutes, until cooked, yet still crunchy. Drain and refresh under cold running water to cool quickly.

4 To make the dressing, mix together the oil, wine vinegar, lemon juice, mustard and sugar. Season well with salt and pepper and add the torn basil leaves.

5 Drain the pasta well and transfer to a large serving bowl. Add the dressing and toss well. Add the (bell) pepper, courgettes (zucchini), onion and cherry tomatoes,

stirring to combine.
Cover and leave at room
temperature for about

30 minutes to allow the
flavours to develop. Serve,
garnished with sprigs of basil.

Vegetable & Pasta Salad

This is delicious served with cold meats.

SERVES 4

2 small aubergines (eggplant), thinly sliced
1 large onion, sliced
2 large beef-steak tomatoes, skinned and cut into wedges
1 red (bell) pepper, cored, deseeded and sliced
1 fennel bulb, thinly sliced • 2 garlic cloves, sliced
4 tbsp olive oil
175 g/6 oz small pasta shapes, such as bows
90 g/3 oz/½ cup Feta cheese, crumbled
a few basil leaves, torn • salt and pepper
salad leaves (greens), to serve

Dressing:
5 tbsp olive oil • juice of 1 orange
1 tsp grated orange zest • ¼ tsp paprika
4 canned anchovies, finely chopped • pepper

1 Place the aubergines (eggplant) in a colander, sprinkle with salt and set aside for about 1 hour to draw out the juices. Rinse under cold, running water to remove the salt, then dry on paper towels.

2 Arrange the aubergines (eggplant), onion, tomatoes, (bell) pepper, fennel and garlic in a single layer in an ovenproof dish, sprinkle on 3 tablespoons of the olive oil and season. Bake uncovered in a preheated oven, 220°C/425°F/Gas Mark 7, for 45 minutes or until the vegetables begin to turn brown. Remove from the oven and set aside to cool.

3 Cook the pasta (see page 59). Transfer the drained pasta to a bowl.

4 To make the dressing, mix together the oil, orange juice and zest and paprika. Stir in the anchovies

and season with pepper. Pour
the dressing over the pasta
while it is hot, and toss well.
Set the pasta aside to cool.

5 To assemble the salad,
line a shallow serving dish
with the salad leaves (greens),
spoon the pasta in a layer
over the leaves, and arrange
the cold roasted vegetables in
the centre. Scatter over the
Feta cheese and basil leaves.
Serve at once.

Spicy Sausage Salad

A warm sausage and pasta dressing spooned over chilled salad leaves makes a refreshing combination with which to start a meal.

SERVES 4

125g/ 4 oz small pasta shapes, such as elbow tubetti
3 tbsp olive oil
1 medium onion, chopped
2 cloves garlic, crushed
1 small yellow (bell) pepper, cored,
seeded and cut into matchsticks
175 g/ 6 oz spicy pork sausage such as chorizo,
skinned and sliced
2 tbsp red wine
1 tbsp red wine vinegar
mixed salad leaves, chilled
salt

1 Cook the pasta as described on page 59. Set aside the drained pasta.

2 Heat 2 tablespoons of the oil in a saucepan over a medium heat. Fry the onion until it is translucent, stir in the garlic, (bell) pepper and sliced sausage and cook for 3–4 minutes, stirring occasionally.

3 Add the wine, wine vinegar and reserved pasta to the pan, stir to blend well and bring the mixture just to the boil.

4 Arrange the chilled salad leaves on 4 individual serving plates and spoon on the warm sausage and pasta mixture. Serve at once.

Seafood Salad

**Seafood is plentiful in Italy and varieties of
seafood salads are found everywhere.**

SERVES 4

175 g/6 oz squid rings, defrosted if frozen
600 ml/1 pint/2½ cups water
150 ml/¼ pint/⅔ cup dry white wine
250 g/8 oz hake or monkfish, cut into cubes
16–20 fresh mussels, scrubbed and beards removed
20 clams in shells, scrubbed, if available
(otherwise use extra mussels)
125–175 g/4–6 oz peeled prawns (shrimp)
3–4 spring onions (scallions), trimmed and sliced (optional)
radicchio and endive (chicory) leaves, to serve
lemon wedges, to garnish

Dressing:
6 tbsp olive oil • 1 tbsp wine vinegar
2 tbsp chopped fresh parsley • 1–2 garlic cloves, crushed
salt and pepper

Garlic mayonnaise:
5 tbsp thick mayonnaise
2–3 tbsp fromage frais or natural yogurt
2 garlic cloves, crushed • 1 tbsp capers
2 tbsp chopped fresh parsley or mixed herbs

1 Poach the squid in the water and wine for 20 minutes or until nearly tender. Add the fish and cook gently for 7–8 minutes or until tender. Strain, reserving the fish. Pour the stock into a clean pan.

2 Bring the fish stock to the boil and add the mussels and clams. Cover the pan and simmer for 5 minutes or until the shells open. Discard any that remain closed. Drain the shellfish and remove from their shells. Put into a bowl

with the cooked fish and add the prawns (shrimp) and spring onions (scallions), if using.

4 Combine all the ingredients for the garlic mayonnaise in a bowl.

3 For the dressing, whisk together the oil, vinegar, parsley, garlic, salt and plenty of black pepper. Pour over the fish, mixing well. Cover and chill for several hours.

5 Arrange small leaves of radicchio and endive on 4 plates and spoon the seafood into the centre. Garnish with lemon wedges and serve with the garlic mayonnaise.

Chargrilled Chicken Salad

This is a quick dish to serve as a starter to your hungry guests. If the bread is bent in half, the chicken salad can be put in the middle and eaten as finger food.

SERVES 4

2 skinless, boneless chicken breasts
1 red onion • oil for brushing
1 avocado, pitted • 1 tbsp lemon juice
120 ml/4 fl oz/½ cup mayonnaise
¼ tsp chilli powder
½ tsp pepper • ¼ tsp salt
4 tomatoes, quartered
1 round sun-dried tomato-flavoured focaccia bread
green salad, to serve

1 Cut the chicken breasts into 1 cm/½ inch strips.

2 Cut the onion into eight pieces, held together at the root. Rinse under cold running water, pat dry and brush with oil.

3 Purée or mash the avocado and lemon juice together. Whisk in the mayonnaise. Add the chilli powder, pepper and salt.

4 Grill (broil) the chicken and onion over a hot barbecue for 3–4 minutes on each side until just beginning to blacken.

5 Combine the blackened chicken and onion with the avocado mixture, then stir in the tomatoes.

6 Cut the focaccia into four quarters, then slice each quarter in half horizontally. Toast on the hot barbecue for about 2 minutes on each side. Spoon the chicken mixture over the toasts and serve with a green salad.

Filled Jacket Potatoes

Wrap the cooked potatoes in foil and keep them warm at the edge of the barbecue, ready to serve with a choice of fillings.

EACH DRESSING SERVES 4

4 large or 8 medium baking potatoes

Mexican sweetcorn relish:
250 g/8 oz can of sweetcorn, drained
½ red (bell) pepper, cored, deseeded and chopped finely
5 cm/2 inch piece of cucumber, chopped finely
½ tsp chilli powder • salt and pepper

Blue cheese, celery & chive filling:
125 g/4 oz/½ cup full-fat soft cheese
125 g/4 oz/½ cup natural fromage frais
125 g/4 oz Danish blue cheese, cut into cubes
1 celery stick, chopped finely
2 tsp snipped fresh chives • celery • salt and pepper

Mushrooms in spicy tomato sauce:
30 g/1 oz/2 tbsp butter or margarine
250 g/8 oz button mushrooms
150 g/5 oz/⅔ cup natural yogurt
1 tbsp tomato purée (paste)
2 tsp mild curry powder • salt and pepper
paprika or chilli powder, or chopped fresh herbs, to garnish

1 Scrub the potatoes and prick them with a fork. Bake in a preheated oven at 200°C/400°F/Gas Mark 6 for about 1 hour, until just tender. Wrap the potatoes in foil and keep warm.

2 To make the Mexican sweetcorn relish, put half the sweetcorn into a bowl. Put the remainder into a blender or food processor and blend for 10–15 seconds or chop and mash roughly by

hand. Add the puréed sweetcorn, (bell) pepper, cucumber and chilli powder to the sweetcorn kernels in the bowl. Season to taste.

3 To make the blue cheese, celery & chive filling, mix the soft cheese and fromage frais together until smooth. Add the blue cheese, celery and chives, and mix. Season with pepper and celery salt.

4 To make the mushrooms in spicy tomato sauce, melt the butter or margarine in a frying pan (skillet). Add the mushrooms and cook gently for 3–4 minutes. Remove from the heat and stir in the yogurt, tomato purée (paste) and curry powder. Season to taste.

5 Serve the potatoes with your choice of fillings and garnish with paprika or herbs.

Melted Cheese & Onion Baguettes

Part-baked baguettes are filled with a cheese and onion mixture, then cooked over the barbecue to make them crisp.

SERVES 4

4 part-baked baguettes • 2 tbsp tomato relish
60 g/2 oz/4 tbsp butter
8 spring onions (scallions), trimmed and chopped finely
125 g/4 oz/½ cup cream cheese
125 g/4 oz/1¾ cups Cheddar cheese, grated
1 tsp snipped fresh chives • pepper

To serve:
mixed salad leaves (greens) • fresh herbs

1 Split the baguettes in half lengthways, without cutting right through. Spread a little tomato relish on each split baguette.

2 Melt the butter in a frying pan (skillet) and add the spring onions (scallions). Fry gently until softened and golden. Remove from the heat and leave to cool slightly.

3 Beat the cream cheese in a mixing bowl to soften it. Mix in the spring onions (scallions), with any remaining butter. Add the grated cheese and snipped chives, mix well and season.

4 Divide the cheese mixture between the baguettes, spread it over the cut surfaces and sandwich together. Wrap each baguette tightly in foil.

5 Heat the baguettes over the barbecue for about 10–15 minutes, turning them occasionally. Peel back the foil to check that they are cooked and the cheese mixture has melted. Serve with salad leaves (greens) and garnished with fresh herbs.

Beef Patties

The traditional beefburger needs no egg to hold it together. Do not be tempted to use extra-lean meat as the result will be too dry; any excess fat will drain off anyway.

SERVES 4

500 g/ 1 lb 2 oz minced (ground) beef
250 g/ 8 oz/ 1 cup minced (ground) lamb
1 onion, chopped finely • 4 soft hamburger buns
½ iceberg lettuce, shredded • 4 gherkins
mustard • salt and pepper

Salsa:

6 tomatoes, halved • 1 red onion, chopped finely
1 red chilli, deseeded and chopped
2 tbsp dark brown sugar
50 ml/ 2 fl oz/ ¼ cup cider vinegar
1 tsp balsamic or sherry vinegar • salt and pepper
2 tbsp chopped fresh chervil (optional)

1 Combine the beef, lamb and onion in a large bowl and season. Divide the mixture into 4 and make 1 ball from each quarter. To ensure that the patties have no air pockets, throw each ball between your cupped hands several times to compact the mixture, until you have a dense ball of meat. Put each ball on a plate and press down gently with the palm of your hand to make it into a patty. Chill.

2 To make the salsa, bake the tomato halves in a preheated oven at 180°C/ 350°F/Gas Mark 4 for 40–50 minutes until collapsed. Chop the tomato coarsely and combine with the onion, chilli, sugar, vinegars and chervil. Season and transfer to a serving dish.

3 Cook the patties over a hot barbecue for 10 minutes, turning once. This will give a medium-rare

burger – for a well-done burger, cook for 15 minutes. Towards the end of cooking time, split the soft hamburger buns and toast lightly on the barbecue for 1–2 minutes on the cut side.

4 Put some shredded lettuce, the beefburger, a gherkin and mustard to taste on the bottom half of the toasted bun, and cover with the top half. Serve with the tomato salsa.

Spaghetti Carbonara

Ensure that all the cooked ingredients are as hot as possible, so that the beaten eggs are cooked on contact.

SERVES 4

400 g/14 oz spaghetti • 2 tbsp olive oil
1 large onion, sliced thinly • 2 garlic cloves, chopped
175 g/6 oz streaky bacon rashers, rind
removed, cut into thin strips
30 g/1 oz/2 tbsp butter
175 g/6 oz mushrooms, sliced thinly
300 ml/½ pint/1¼ cups double (heavy) cream
3 eggs, beaten
90 g/3 oz/1 cup Parmesan, grated,
plus extra to serve (optional)
salt and pepper • sprigs of sage, to garnish

1 Cook the spaghetti as described on page 11. Return the drained spaghetti to the pan, cover and keep warm.

2 Heat the remaining oil in a frying pan (skillet) over a medium heat. Fry the onion until it is translucent, then add the garlic and bacon and fry until the bacon is crisp. Remove the onion, garlic and bacon with a slotted spoon and set aside to keep warm. Heat the butter in the pan, add the mushrooms and fry for 3–4 minutes, stirring occasionally. Return the bacon mixture to the pan with the mushrooms. Cover and keep warm.

3 Mix the cream, beaten eggs and cheese in a bowl, and season with salt and pepper.

4 Working quickly, tip the spaghetti into the bacon and mushroom mixture and pour on the eggs. Toss the spaghetti quickly, using 2 forks, and serve hot, with extra grated Parmesan, if liked.

Spaghetti Bolognese

This familiar meat sauce, known as ragù, may also be used in lasagne.

SERVES 4

400 g/14 oz spaghetti • *1 tbsp olive oil* • *salt*
15 g/½ oz/1 tbsp butter
2 tbsp chopped fresh parsley, to garnish

Ragù:

3 tbsp olive oil • *45 g/1½ oz/3 tbsp butter*
2 large onions, chopped • *4 celery stalks, sliced thinly*
175 g/6 oz streaky bacon, chopped into small strips
2 garlic cloves, chopped
500 g/1 lb 2 oz minced (ground) lean beef
2 tbsp tomato purée (paste) • *1 tbsp flour*
400 g/14 oz can of chopped tomatoes
150 ml/¼ pint/⅔ cup beef stock
150 ml/¼ pint/⅔ cup red wine • *2 tsp dried oregano*
½ tsp freshly grated nutmeg • *salt and pepper*

1 To make the ragù: heat the oil and the butter in a large frying pan (skillet) over a medium heat. Add the onions, celery and bacon pieces and fry for 5 minutes, stirring occasionally

2 Stir in the garlic and minced (ground) beef and cook, stirring, until the meat has lost its redness. Lower the heat and continue cooking for a further 10 minutes, stirring occasionally

3 Increase the heat to medium, stir in the tomato purée (paste) and the flour and cook for 1–2 minutes. Stir in the chopped tomatoes, beef stock and wine, and bring to the boil, stirring. Season with salt and pepper and stir in the oregano and nutmeg. Cover the pan and simmer for 45 minutes, stirring occasionally.

4 Cook the spaghetti as described on page 11.

Return the drained pasta to the pan. Dot the spaghetti with the butter and toss thoroughly.

5 Pour the sauce over the spaghetti and toss well. Garnish with the parsley and serve immediately.

Tagliatelle with Meatballs

There is an appetizing contrast of textures and flavours in this satisfying family dish.

SERVES 4

500 g/1 lb 2 oz minced (ground) lean beef
60 g/2 oz/1 cup soft white breadcrumbs
1 garlic clove, crushed • 2 tbsp chopped fresh parsley
1 tsp dried oregano • large pinch of freshly grated nutmeg
¼ tsp ground coriander
60 g/2 oz/¾ cup Parmesan, grated • 2–3 tbsp milk
flour, for dusting • 5 tbsp olive oil
400 g/14 oz tagliatelli • 30 g/1 oz/2 tbsp butter, diced
salt • mixed salad, to serve

Sauce:
3 tbsp olive oil • 2 large onions, sliced
2 celery stalks, sliced thinly • 2 garlic cloves, chopped
400 g/14 oz can of chopped tomatoes
125 g/4 oz bottled sun-dried tomatoes, drained and chopped
2 tbsp tomato purée (paste) • 1 tbsp dark muscovado sugar
150 ml/¼ pint/⅔ cup white wine, or water
salt and pepper

1 To make the sauce, heat the oil in a pan and fry the onion and celery until translucent. Add the garlic and cook for 1 minute. Stir in the tomatoes, tomato purée (paste), sugar and wine, and season. Bring to the boil and simmer for 10 minutes.

2 Break up the meat in a bowl with a wooden spoon until it becomes a sticky paste. Stir in the breadcrumbs, garlic, herbs and spices. Stir in the cheese and enough milk to make a firm paste. Flour your hands, take large spoonfuls of the mixture and shape it into 12 balls. Heat 4 tablespoons of the oil in a frying pan (skillet) and fry the meatballs for 5–6 minutes until browned.

3 Pour the tomato sauce over the meatballs. Lower the heat, cover the pan and simmer for 30 minutes, turning occasionally. Add a little extra water if the sauce begins to dry out.

4 Cook the pasta as described on page 11. Turn into a warmed serving dish, dot with the butter and toss with two forks. Spoon the meatballs and sauce over the pasta and sprinkle on the parsley. Serve with a mixed salad.

Sausages

Sausages are always one of the most popular things at a barbecue. Here is how to get a good result.

SERVES 4

4 barbecue pork sausages, the double-length kind, or 8 standard size sausages
olive oil for brushing

To serve:
1 onion
1 French baguette, cut into 4
French mustard

1 Prick the sausages all over with a fork. This not only ensures that the skin does not split, but also allows the excess fat to run out. Pork and beef sausages work very well on a barbecue as they are quite firm. Brush the sausages all over with oil – this also protects the skin.

2 Cook the sausages over a hot barbecue for 10 minutes, turning frequently. If you are using standard-sized pork sausages, they will cook in less time, and chipolatas will only take 5–7 minutes.

3 Cut the onion into 8 pieces, each piece held together by a bit of onion root. Brush with oil and cook over the barbecue for 2–3 minutes.

4 Meanwhile, insert a bread knife inside each piece of baguette. Without breaking the crust, hollow out enough bread for the sausage to fit in.

5 Spread a line of mustard through the middle of the bread. Put 2 pieces of onion in each piece of baguette and push the cooked sausage through the middle. If using standard-sized sausages, put one in each end.

Devilled New Potatoes

This is a way of giving potatoes, or any other root vegetable you have to hand, the star treatment. A barbecue needs smaller side dishes like this to keep your diners happy while they wait for the main event.

SERVES 6–8

20 cocktail sticks (toothpicks)
500 g/1 lb 2 oz baby new potatoes
olive oil for brushing
10 rashers (slices) streaky bacon
20 small sage leaves

1 Soak the cocktail sticks (toothpicks) in hand-hot water for 20 minutes before using. This will prevent them from scorching during cooking.

2 Bring a pan of water to the boil and add the potatoes. Boil for 10 minutes and drain. Brush the potatoes all over with olive oil.

3 Cut each bacon rasher (slice) in half along its length. Holding each piece at one end, smooth and stretch it with the back of a knife.

4 Wrap a piece of bacon around each potato enclosing a sage leaf and securing with a cocktail stick (toothpick).

5 Cook the potatoes over a hot barbecue for 6–7 minutes, turning occasionally. Serve hot or cold.

Stuffed Red (Bell) Peppers

Stuffed (bell) peppers are a well-known dish, but this is a new version adapted for the barbecue. The roasted vegetables have a tasty Mediterranean flavour.

SERVES 4

2 red (bell) peppers, halved lengthways and deseeded
2 tomatoes, halved
2 courgettes (zucchini), sliced thinly lengthways
1 red onion, cut into 8 sections, each section held together by the root
4 tbsp olive oil
2 tbsp fresh thyme leaves
60 g / 2 oz / ⅓ cup mixed basmati and wild rice, cooked
salt and pepper

1 Put the halved (bell) peppers, halved tomatoes, sliced courgettes (zucchini) and onion sections on to a baking (cookie) sheet.

2 Brush the vegetables with olive oil and sprinkle over the thyme leaves.

3 Cook the (bell) pepper, onion and courgette (zucchini) over a medium-hot barbecue for 6 minutes, turning once.

4 When the (bell) peppers are cooked, put a spoonful of the cooked rice into each one, and place the onion and courgette (zucchini) on top.

5 Cook the tomato halves for 2–3 minutes only. Top each stuffed (bell) pepper with a tomato half. Season with plenty of salt and pepper and serve hot.

Tortellini

**According to legend, tortellini resembles
Venus's navel.**

SERVES 4

125 g/ 4 oz boned and skinned chicken breast
60 g/ 2 oz Parma ham (prosciutto)
45 g/ 1½ oz cooked spinach, well drained
1 tbsp finely chopped onion • 2 tbsp freshly grated Parmesan
good pinch of ground allspice • 1 egg, beaten • salt and pepper

Pasta dough:
125 g/ 4 oz/ 1 cup strong plain (all-purpose) flour
125 g/ 4 oz/ ⅔ cup fine semolina • 1 tsp salt
2 tbsp olive oil • 2 eggs • 2–3 tbsp hot water

Sauce:
300 ml/ ½ pint/ 1¼ cups single (light) cream
1–2 garlic cloves, crushed
125 g/ 4 oz button mushrooms, sliced thinly
4 tbsp freshly grated Parmesan • 1–2 tbsp chopped parsley

1 Poach the chicken in well-seasoned water until tender, about 10 minutes; drain and chop roughly. When cool put into a food processor with the Parma ham (prosciutto), spinach and onion and process until finely chopped. Stir in the Parmesan, allspice, seasonings and egg.

2 To make the pasta dough, sieve the flour, semolina and salt into a bowl and make a well in the centre. Pour in the oil and add the eggs. Add 1 tablespoon of hot water and work to a dough with your fingertips, adding water if necessary to make it more pliable. Turn the dough on to a floured board and knead it for 10–12 minutes until elastic and smooth.

3 Roll out the pasta dough, half at a time, on a lightly floured surface until as thin as

74

possible. Cut into 5 cm/ 2 inch rounds using a plain cutter. Place $^1/_2$ teaspoon of the filling in the centre of each dough circle, fold the pieces in half to make a semi-circle and press the edges firmly together. Wrap the semi-circle around your index finger and cross over the two ends, pressing firmly together, curling the dough backwards to make a 'tummy button' shape. Lay the tortellini on a lightly floured tray. Repeat with the rest of the dough, re-rolling the trimmings.

4 Heat a large pan of salted boiling water and add a few tortellini. Bring back to the boil and once they rise to the surface cook for about 5 minutes, giving an occasional stir. Remove with a slotted spoon and drain on paper towels. Keep warm in a dish.

5 To make the sauce, heat the cream with the garlic in a pan and bring to the boil. Simmer for a few minutes. Add the mushrooms, half the Parmesan and salt and pepper to taste, and simmer for 2–3 minutes. Stir in the parsley and pour over the warm tortellini. Sprinkle with the remaining Parmesan and serve at once.

Stuffed Cannelloni

Cannelloni make perfect containers for close-textured sauces of all kinds.

SERVES 4

8 cannelloni tubes • 1 tbsp olive oil
30 g/1 oz /½ cup Parmesan, grated
fresh herb sprigs, to garnish

Filling:
30 g/1 oz/2 tbsp butter
300 g/10 oz frozen spinach, defrosted and chopped
125 g/4 oz /¾ cup Ricotta
30 g/1 oz/½ cup Parmesan, grated
60 g/2 oz/¼ cup chopped ham
¼ tsp freshly grated nutmeg • 2 tbsp double (heavy) cream
2 eggs, lightly beaten • salt and pepper

Sauce:
30 g/1 oz/2 tbsp butter • 30 g/1 oz/¼ cup flour
300 ml/½ pint/1¼ cups milk • 2 bay leaves
large pinch of grated nutmeg • salt and pepper

1 To make the filling, melt the butter in a pan and stir in the spinach. Stir for 2–3 minutes, then remove the pan from the heat. Stir in the cheeses and the ham. Season with nutmeg, and salt and pepper. Beat in the cream and eggs to make a thick paste. Set aside to cool.

2 Cook the cannelloni in a large pan of boiling salted water, adding the olive oil. When almost tender, after 10–12 minutes, drain and set aside to cool.

3 To make the sauce, melt the butter in a pan, stir in the flour and, when it has formed a *roux*, gradually pour on the milk, stirring all the time. Add the bay leaves, bring to simmering point, and cook for 5 minutes. Season

with nutmeg, salt and pepper. Remove from the heat and discard the bay leaves.

4 Spoon the filling into a piping bag and pipe it into each of the cannelloni tubes. Spoon a little of the sauce into a shallow baking dish. Arrange the cannelloni in a single layer, then pour over the remaining sauce. Sprinkle with Parmesan cheese and bake in a preheated oven, 190°C/ 375°F/Gas Mark 5, for 40–45 minutes, until the sauce is golden brown and bubbling. Serve garnished with fresh herb sprigs.

Tagliatelle with Pumpkin

This unusual pasta dish comes from the Emilia Romagna region.

SERVES 4

500 g/ 1 lb 2 oz pumpkin or butternut squash
2 tbsp olive oil • 1 onion, chopped finely
2 garlic cloves, crushed • 4–6 tbsp chopped fresh parsley
good pinch of ground or freshly grated nutmeg
about 250 ml/ 8 fl oz/ 1 cup chicken or vegetable stock
125 g/ 4 oz Parma ham (prosciutto), cut into narrow strips
275 g/ 9 oz tagliatelle, green or white (fresh or dried)
150 ml/ ¼ pint/ ⅔ cup double (heavy) cream
salt and pepper • freshly grated Parmesan, to serve

1 Peel the pumpkin or butternut squash and scoop out the seeds and membrane. Cut the flesh into 1 cm/½ inch dice.

2 Heat the oil in a pan and gently fry the onion and garlic until soft. Add half the parsley and fry for 1–2 minutes. Add the squash or pumpkin and continue to cook for 2–3 minutes. Season well with salt, pepper and nutmeg. Add half the stock, bring to the boil, cover and simmer for about 10 minutes or until the pumpkin is tender, adding more stock as necessary. Add the Parma ham (prosciutto) and continue to cook for 2 minutes, stirring frequently.

3 Meanwhile, cook the tagliatelle in a large saucepan of boiling salted water, allowing 3–4 minutes for fresh pasta or 12 minutes for dried (or follow the directions on the packet). When tender but still with some bite, drain thoroughly and turn into a warmed dish.

4 Add the cream to the ham mixture and heat gently until really hot. Adjust the seasoning and spoon over the pasta. Sprinkle with the remaining parsley and the grated Parmesan.

Tomato & Courgette (Zucchini) Frittata

A frittata is a type of Italian omelette thick with a variety of vegetables, fish or meat. You can add almost anything to the eggs. It is also delicious eaten cold (but not chilled) and makes an ideal picnic dish.

SERVES 4

3 tbsp olive oil
1 onion, chopped
2 garlic cloves, chopped
250 g/8 oz courgettes (zucchini), sliced thinly
4 eggs
400 g/14 oz can borlotti beans, drained and rinsed
3 tomatoes, skinned and chopped
2 tbsp chopped fresh parsley
1 tbsp chopped fresh basil
60 g/2 oz/½ cup Gruyère (Swiss) cheese, grated
salt and pepper

1 Heat 2 tablespoons of the oil in a frying pan (skillet) and fry the onion and garlic stirring occasionally, until soft. Add the courgettes (zucchini) and cook until softened.

2 Break the eggs into a bowl and add the salt and pepper, fried vegetables, beans, tomatoes and herbs.

3 Heat the remaining oil in a 24 cm/9½ inch omelette pan, add the egg mixture and fry gently for 5 minutes until the eggs have almost set and the underside is brown.

4 Sprinkle the cheese over the top and place the pan under a preheated moderate grill (broiler) for 3–4 minutes until set on the top but still moist in the middle. Cut into wedges and serve warm or at room temperature.

Gnocchi Romana

**This is a traditional recipe from Piedmont.
For a less rich version, omit the eggs. Serve
as a starter, or a main meal with a salad.**

SERVES 4

750 ml/ 1¼ pints/ 3 cups milk
¼ tsp freshly grated nutmeg
90 g/ 3 oz/ 6 tbsp butter, plus extra for greasing
250 g/ 8 oz/ 1⅓ cups semolina
125 g/ 4 oz/ 1¾ cups Parmesan, grated
2 eggs, beaten • 60 g/ 2 oz/¾ cup Gruyère, grated
salt and pepper
basil sprigs, to garnish

1 Bring the milk to the boil, remove from the heat and stir in the salt and pepper, nutmeg and 30 g/1 oz/ 2 tablespoons of butter. Gradually add the semolina, whisking to prevent lumps forming, and return to a low heat. Simmer gently for about 10 minutes, stirring constantly, until very thick. Beat 60 g/2 oz/½ cup of Parmesan into the semolina, followed by the eggs. Continue beating until the mixture is quite smooth.

2 Spread out the semolina mixture in an even layer about 1 cm/½ inch thick on a sheet of baking parchment or in a large oiled baking tin (pan), smoothing the surface with a wet spatula. Leave until cold, then chill for about 1 hour or until firm. Cut the gnocchi into circles about 4 cm/1½ inches in diameter, using a greased plain pastry cutter.

3 Thoroughly grease a shallow ovenproof dish, or 4 individual dishes. Lay the gnocchi trimmings in the base of the dish and cover with overlapping circles of gnocchi. Melt the remaining butter and drizzle all over the gnocchi, then sprinkle first with the remaining Parmesan and then with the Gruyère.

4 Cook the gnocchi in a preheated oven, 200°C/ 400°F/Gas Mark 6, for 25–30 minutes until the top is golden brown. Serve hot, garnished with basil sprigs.

Polenta

**Polenta is prepared in a variety of ways
and can be hot or cold, sweet or savoury.**

SERVES 4

*1.5 litres/ 2⅓ pints/ 7 cups water • 1½ tsp salt
300 g/ 10 oz/ 2 cups polenta or cornmeal flour
2 beaten eggs (optional)
125 g/ 4 oz/ 2 cups fresh fine white
breadcrumbs (optional)
vegetable oil, for frying and oiling*

Tomato sauce:

*2 tbsp olive oil • 1 small onion, chopped
1 garlic clove, chopped
400 g/ 14 oz can of chopped tomatoes
2 tbsp chopped parsley • 1 tsp dried oregano
2 bay leaves • 2 tbsp tomato purée (paste)
1 tsp sugar • salt and pepper*

1 Bring the water and salt to the boil in a large pan and gradually sprinkle in the polenta or cornmeal flour, stirring all the time to prevent lumps forming. Simmer very gently, stirring frequently, until the polenta becomes very thick and starts to draw away from the sides of the pan, about 30–35 minutes. It is likely to splatter, in which case partially cover the pan.

2 Thoroughly oil a shallow tin, about 28 × 18 cm/ 11 × 7 inches, and spoon in the polenta. Spread out evenly, using a wet spatula. Allow to cool, then leave to stand for a few hours at room temperature, if possible.

3 Cut the polenta into 30–36 squares. Heat the oil in a frying pan (skillet) and fry the pieces until golden brown all over, turning several times – about 5 minutes. Alternatively, dip each piece of polenta in beaten egg and coat in

breadcrumbs before frying in the hot oil.

4 To make the tomato sauce, heat the oil in a pan over a medium heat and fry the onion until soft. Add the garlic and fry for 1 minute. Stir in the chopped tomatoes, parsley, oregano, bay leaves, tomato purée (paste), sugar, salt and pepper. Bring the sauce to the boil, then simmer, uncovered, for 15–20 minutes until it has reduced by half. Adjust the seasoning if necessary. Discard the bay leaves. Serve the polenta with the tomato sauce.

Milanese Risotto

Italian rice is a round, short-grained variety with a nutty flavour, which is essential for a good risotto. Arborio is a good one to use.

SERVES 4

2 good pinches of saffron threads
1 large onion, chopped finely
1–2 garlic cloves, crushed
90 g/ 3 oz/ 6 tbsp butter
350 g/ 12 oz/ 1²/₃ cups Arborio or other
short-grain Italian rice
150 ml/ ¼ pint/ ²/₃ cup dry white wine
1.25 litres/ 2¼ pints/ 5 cups boiling stock
(chicken, beef or vegetable)
90 g/ 3 oz/ 1¼ cups Parmesan, grated
salt and pepper

1 Put the saffron in a small bowl, cover with 3–4 tablespoons of boiling water and leave to soak while cooking the risotto.

2 Fry the onion and garlic in 60 g/2 oz/ 4 tablespoons of the butter until soft but not coloured, then add the rice and continue to cook for a few minutes until all the grains are coated in butter and just beginning to colour. Add the wine to the rice and simmer gently, stirring occasionally until it is all absorbed.

Add the boiling stock a little at a time, about 150 ml/ ¼ pint/²/₃ cup, cooking until the liquid is absorbed before adding more, and stirring frequently.

3 When all the stock is absorbed the rice should be tender but not soft. Add the saffron liquid, Parmesan, remaining butter and plenty of seasoning. Simmer for 1–2 minutes until piping hot and thoroughly mixed. Cover the pan and leave to stand for 5 minutes off the heat. Stir and serve at once.

Poultry & Meat

This chapter features exciting ways of cooking poultry and meat to offer a variety of satisfying meals. Dishes range from easy, economical mid-week suppers to sophisticated and elegant meals for special occasions. There are also tempting recipes to liven up a summer barbecue.

Chicken Scallops

**Served in scallop shells, this dish makes
a stylish presentation for a dinner-party
first course.**

SERVES 4

175 g/ 6 oz short-cut macaroni, or other short pasta shapes
3 tbsp vegetable oil, plus extra for brushing
1 medium onion, finely chopped
*3 rashers unsmoked collar or back bacon,
rind removed, chopped*
125 g/ 4 oz button mushrooms, thinly sliced or chopped
175 g/ 6 oz cooked chicken, diced
175 ml/ 6 fl oz/ ³⁄₄ cup crème fraîche
4 tbsp dry breadcrumbs
60 g/ 2 oz/ ³⁄₄ cup mature (sharp) Cheddar cheese, grated
salt and pepper
flat-leaved parsley sprigs, to garnish

1 Cook the pasta as described on page 11. Return the drained pasta to the pan and cover.

2 Heat the grill (broiler) to medium. Heat the remaining oil in a pan over a medium heat and fry the onion until it is translucent. Add the chopped bacon and mushrooms and cook for 3–4 minutes, stirring occasionally. Stir in the pasta, chicken and crème fraîche and season with salt and pepper.

3 Brush 4 large scallop shells with oil. Spoon in the chicken mixture and smooth to make neat mounds.

4 Mix together the breadcrumbs and cheese and sprinkle over the top of the shells. Press the topping lightly into the chicken mixture, and grill (broil) for 4–5 minutes, until golden brown and bubbling. Garnish with parsley sprigs, and serve hot.

Tagliatelle with Chicken

Spinach ribbon noodles covered with a rich tomato sauce and topped with creamy chicken makes this a very appetizing dish.

SERVES 4

Tomato Sauce (page 10)
250 g/ 8 oz fresh green ribbon noodles
1 tbsp olive oil
salt
basil leaves, to garnish

Chicken sauce:
60 g/ 2 oz/ 4 tbsp unsalted butter
400 g/ 14 oz boned, skinned chicken breast, thinly sliced
90 g/ 3 oz/ ½ cup blanched almonds
300 ml/ ½ pint/ 1¼ cups double (heavy) cream
salt and pepper

1 Make the tomato sauce, and keep warm.

2 To make the chicken sauce, melt the butter in a pan over a medium heat and fry the chicken strips and almonds for 5–6 minutes, stirring frequently, until the chicken is cooked through.

3 Meanwhile, pour the cream into a small pan over a low heat, bring it to the boil and boil for about 10 minutes, until reduced by almost half. Pour the cream over the chicken and almonds, stir well, and season. Set aside and keep warm.

4 Cook the pasta as described on page 11. Return the drained pasta to the saucepan, cover and keep warm.

5 Turn the pasta into a warmed serving dish and spoon over the tomato sauce. Spoon the chicken and cream over the centre, scatter the basil leaves and serve at once.

Filipino Chicken

**Tomato ketchup is used in this recipe
from the Philippines. It is a very
popular ingredient as it has a zingy
sweet-sour flavour.**

SERVES 4

1 can of lemonade or lime-and-lemonade
2 tbsp gin
4 tbsp tomato ketchup
2 tsp garlic salt
2 tsp Worcestershire sauce
4 chicken supremes or breasts
salt and pepper

To serve:
thread egg noodles
1 green chilli, chopped finely
2 spring onions (scallions), sliced

1 Combine the lemonade or
lime-and-lemonade, gin,
tomato ketchup, garlic salt,
Worcestershire sauce and
seasoning in a large non-
porous dish.

2 Add the chicken pieces to
the dish, ensuring they
are covered completely.

3 Cover and put in the
refrigerator to marinate
for 2 hours. Allow to come to
room temperature for 30
minutes before cooking.

4 Cook the chicken over
a medium-hot barbecue
for 20 minutes, turning
once, until completely
cooked through.

5 Remove the chicken from
the barbecue and leave to
rest for 3–4 minutes.

6 Carve into thin slices and
serve with egg noodles,
tossed with a little green chilli
and spring onions (scallions).

Mediterranean Grilled Chicken

This recipe from the Languedoc area of France uses crisp, juicy chicken.

SERVES 4

4 tbsp natural yogurt
3 tbsp sun-dried tomato paste
1 tbsp olive oil
15 g/½ oz/¼ cup fresh basil leaves, lightly crushed
2 garlic cloves, roughly chopped
4 chicken quarters
coarse sea salt
green salad, to serve

1 Combine the yogurt, tomato paste, olive oil, basil leaves and garlic in a small bowl and mix well.

2 Put the marinade into a bowl large enough to hold the chicken quarters in a single layer. Add the chicken quarters, making sure they are thoroughly coated in the marinade.

3 Leave the chicken to marinate in the refrigerator for at least 2 hours or overnight. Remove and leave, covered, at room temperature for 30 minutes before cooking.

4 Grill (broil) the chicken over a medium-hot barbecue for 30–40 minutes, turning frequently.

5 Check the meat is cooked by piercing the flesh at the top of the drumstick. If the juices run clear, the chicken is cooked. If the juices are pink, cook for another 10 minutes.

6 Sprinkle with coarse sea salt and serve hot or cold with a green salad.

Blackened Chicken with Guacamole

This easy recipe is typical of French Cajun cooking which has its roots in earthy, strong flavours, and uses plenty of spices.

SERVES 4

4 skinless, boneless chicken breasts
60 g/2 oz/4 tbsp butter, melted

Spice mix:

1 tsp salt • 1 tbsp sweet paprika
1 tsp dried onion granules
1 tsp dried garlic granules
1 tsp dried thyme • 1 tsp cayenne pepper
½ tsp cracked black pepper • ½ tsp dried oregano

Guacamole:

1 avocado • 1 tbsp lemon juice • 2 tbsp soured cream
½ red onion, chopped • 1 garlic clove, halved

1 Put the chicken breasts between two pieces of clingfilm (plastic wrap), and pound with a mallet or rolling pin to an even thickness. They should be about 1 cm/½ inch thick. Brush each chicken breast all over with the melted butter, then set aside.

2 Combine the spice mix ingredients in a bowl. Dip the chicken breasts in the spice mix, ensuring that they are well coated. Set aside.

3 To make the guacamole, mash the avocado with the lemon juice in a small bowl. Stir in the soured cream and onion. Wipe the garlic clove around the guacamole serving dish, pressing hard. Spoon in the guacamole.

4 Cook the chicken breasts over the hottest part of a

very hot barbecue for
8–10 minutes, turning
once. Slice the breasts into
thick pieces and serve
immediately, accompanied
by the guacamole.

Tasmanian Duck

Some of the best cherries in the world are grown in Tasmania, hence the name of this recipe, though dried cherries from any country can be used.

SERVES 4

4 duck breasts • 60 g/ 2 oz/ ½ cup dried cherries
120 ml/ 4 fl oz/ ½ cup water • 4 tbsp lemon juice
2 large leeks, quartered, or 8 baby leeks
2 tbsp olive oil • 2 tbsp balsamic vinegar
2 tbsp port • 2 tsp pink peppercorns

1 Make 3 slashes in the fat of the duck breasts in one direction, and 3 in the other.

2 Put the dried cherries, water and lemon juice into a small saucepan. Bring to the boil. Remove from the heat and leave to cool.

3 Turn a foil tray upside-down, make several holes in the bottom and place it, right side up, over a hot barbecue.

4 Put the duck into the tray. Cover with foil and cook for 20 minutes.

5 Brush the leeks with oil and cook on the open barbecue for 5–7 minutes, turning constantly.

6 Remove the duck from the tray and cook on the open barbecue for 5 minutes, skin-side down, while you make the sauce.

7 Stir the balsamic vinegar into the cooking sauces in the tray, scraping any bits from the bottom. Add to the cherries in the saucepan. Return to the heat – either the hob (stove top) or barbecue – and stir in the port and pink peppercorns. Bring to the boil and cook for 5 minutes, until the sauce has thickened slightly.

8 Serve the duck piping hot, pour over the cherries and sauce, and accompany with the leeks.

Chicken with Green Olives

Olives are a popular flavouring for poultry in Apulia, where this recipe originates.

SERVES 4

4 chicken breasts, part boned
30 g / 1 oz / 2 tbsp butter • 2 tbsp olive oil
1 large onion, chopped finely • 2 garlic cloves, crushed
2 red, yellow or green (bell) peppers, cored, deseeded
and cut into large pieces
250 g / 8 oz large closed cup mushrooms, sliced or quartered
175 g / 6 oz tomatoes, peeled and halved
150 ml / ¼ pint / ⅔ cup dry white wine
125–175 g / 4–6 oz green olives, pitted
4–6 tbsp double (heavy) cream
salt and pepper • chopped flat-leaf parsley, to garnish

1 Season the chicken with salt and pepper. Heat the oil and butter in a frying pan (skillet), add the chicken and fry until browned all over. Remove from the pan. Add the onion and garlic to the pan and fry gently until they start to soften. Add the (bell) peppers to the pan with the mushrooms and cook for 2–3 minutes. Add the tomatoes and plenty of seasoning and then transfer the vegetable mixture to an ovenproof casserole. Place the chicken on the bed of vegetables.

2 Add the wine to the frying pan and bring to the boil. Pour over the chicken and cover. Cook in a preheated oven, 180°C / 350°F / Gas Mark 4, for 50 minutes. Add the olives, mix lightly, then pour on the cream. Re-cover the casserole and return to the oven for 10–20 minutes or until the chicken is tender.

3 Adjust the seasoning and serve the chicken breasts, surrounded by the vegetables and sauce, with pasta or new potatoes. Garnish with parsley.

Provençale Grilled Beef

This recipe makes use of a coarse-grained but very tasty cut of beef called a hanging skirt, rump skirt or butcher's cut. You will find that it is very reasonably priced.

SERVES 6–8

1 kg/ 2 lb rump skirt or rump steak
½ tsp pepper
4 tbsp French olive oil
6 anchovies, chopped finely
2 garlic cloves, chopped finely
2 tbsp chopped fresh flat-leafed (Italian) parsley
2 tsp sea salt
French bread, to serve

1 With a sharp knife, trim any excess fat from the meat. Pare off any membrane or connective tissue, which will misshape the meat as it cooks.

2 Rub pepper and 1 tbsp of the olive oil all over the meat. Cover and chill for about 2 hours.

3 Combine the anchovies, garlic, parsley, sea salt and the remaining olive oil.

4 Remove the meat from the refrigerator 30 minutes before cooking.

5 Place the meat over a hot barbecue. Cook for 8 minutes, then turn over and spread the anchovy mix on the top side. Cook the other side for 6 minutes.

6 When the meat is cooked, transfer to a chopping board. Leave to rest for 1 minute before slicing thinly.

7 Transfer to a warmed serving platter and serve with the French bread.

Calabrian Pizza

Traditionally, this pizza has two layers of dough to make it filling. It can also be made as a single pizza, as shown here.

SERVES 4–6

400 g/14 oz/3½ cups plain (all-purpose) flour
½ tsp salt • 1 sachet easy-blend yeast
2 tbsp olive oil
about 275 ml/9 fl oz/generous 1 cup warm water

Filling:
2 tbsp olive oil • 2 garlic cloves, crushed
1 red (bell) pepper, cored, deseeded and sliced
1 yellow (bell) pepper, cored, deseeded and sliced
125 g/4 oz Ricotta
175 g/6 oz jar of sun-dried tomatoes, drained
3 hard-boiled (hard-cooked) eggs, sliced thinly
1 tbsp chopped fresh mixed herbs
125 g/4 oz salami, cut into strips
150–175 g/5–6 oz Mozzarella, grated
a little milk, to glaze • salt and pepper

1 Sift the flour and salt into a bowl and mix in the easy-blend yeast. Add the olive oil and enough warm water to mix to a smooth pliable dough. Knead for 10–15 minutes by hand, or process for 5 minutes in a mixer. Shape the dough into a ball, place in a lightly oiled plastic bag and leave in a warm place for 1–1½ hours.

2 For the filling: heat the oil in a frying pan (skillet) and fry the garlic and (bell) peppers in the oil until soft.

3 Knock back the dough and roll out half to fit the base of a 30 × 25 cm/ 12 × 10 inch oiled roasting tin (pan). Season and spread with the Ricotta. Cover with the sun-dried tomatoes, eggs, herbs and pepper mixture.

Arrange the salami strips on top and sprinkle with the grated cheese. Roll out the remaining dough and place over the filling, sealing the edges well, or use to make a second pizza. Leave to rise for 1 hour in a warm place – uncovered pizzas take only 30–40 minutes to rise.

4 Prick the double pizza with a fork about 20 times, brush the top with milk and cook in a preheated oven, 180°C/350°F/Gas Mark 4, for 50 minutes or until lightly browned. The uncovered pizza will take 35–40 minutes. Serve hot.

Steak in Red Wine Marinade

The steak should be between 2.5 cm/1 inch and 7 cm/3 inches thick. Fillet, sirloin and entrecôte are also suitable, although rump retains the most flavour.

SERVES 4

4 rump steaks, weighing about 250 g/8 oz each
600 ml/1 pint/2½ cups red wine
1 onion, quartered • 2 tbsp Dijon mustard
2 garlic cloves, crushed
4 large field mushrooms
olive oil for brushing • salt and pepper
branch of fresh rosemary (optional)

1 Snip through the fat strip on the steaks in 3 places, so that the steak retains its shape when barbecued.

2 Combine the red wine, onion, mustard, garlic, and salt and pepper. Lay the steaks in a shallow non-porous dish and pour over the marinade. Cover and chill for 2–3 hours.

3 Remove the steaks from the refrigerator 30 minutes before you intend to cook them to let them come to room temperature. This is especially important if the steak is thick, to ensure that it cooks more evenly and is not well done on the outside and raw in the middle.

4 Sear both sides of the steak – about 1 minute on each side – over a hot barbecue. If it is about 2.5 cm/1 inch thick, keep it over a hot barbecue, and cook for about 4 minutes on each side. This will give a medium-rare steak – cook it more or less, to suit your taste. (If the steak is a thicker cut that needs thorough cooking, move it to a less hot part of the barbecue or further away

from the coals and complete cooking.) To test the readiness of the meat while cooking, simply press it with your finger – the more the meat yields, the less it is cooked.

5 Brush the mushrooms with the olive oil and cook them alongside the steak, for 5 minutes, turning once. When you put the mushrooms on the barbecue, put the rosemary branch, if using, on the fire to flavour the meat slightly. Remove the steak and leave to rest for 1–2 minutes before serving. Slice the mushrooms and serve alongside the steak.

Lamb Fillet with Roasted Baby Onions

This dish should be marinated overnight to tenderize the lamb. It also ensures that the flavours seep into the meat and keep it moist during cooking.

SERVES 6–8

500 g/ 1 lb 2 oz lamb neck fillet
500 g/ 1 lb 2 oz pickling (pearl) onions
1 tbsp olive oil • 3 tbsp chopped fresh thyme
2 lemons, rinsed and sliced thickly

Marinade:
4 tbsp olive oil • 3 garlic cloves, well crushed
½ tsp salt • ½ tsp pepper

1 To make the marinade, mix all of the ingredients together to form a paste. Smear the paste all over the lamb fillet and leave to marinate overnight in the refrigerator.

2 Cook the onions in a saucepan of boiling water for 15 minutes, until almost cooked through. Peel them.

3 Heat the oil and thyme in a frying pan (skillet) and add the onions to reheat them and coat them in the oil and thyme. Set aside.

4 Lay the lemon slices over a very hot barbecue. Place the lamb on top and cook for 10 minutes on each side, basting frequently.

5 Meanwhile, put the onions on the grid around the lamb and cook for 10 minutes, turning often until they are quite soft but charred on the outside. Serve the lamb with the onions.

Aubergine (Eggplant) Cake

Layers of toasty-brown aubergine (eggplant), meat sauce and cheese-flavoured pasta.

SERVES 4

1 aubergine (eggplant), sliced thinly • 5 tbsp olive oil
250 g/ 8 oz short pasta shapes, such as fusilli
60 g/ 2 oz/ 4 tbsp butter, plus extra for greasing
45 g/ 1½ oz/ ⅓ cup flour • 300 ml/ ½ pint/ 1¼ cups milk
150 ml/ ¼ pint/ ⅔ cup single (light) cream
150 ml/ ¼ pint/ ⅔ cup chicken stock
large pinch of freshly grated nutmeg
90 g/ 3 oz/ 1¼ cups mature (sharp) Cheddar, grated
Lamb Sauce (page 11) • 30 g/ 1 oz/ ½ cup Parmesan, grated
salt and pepper • artichoke heart and tomato salad, to serve

1 Put the aubergine (eggplant) slices in a colander, sprinkle with salt and leave for 45 minutes. Rinse under cold running water and dry with paper towels. Heat 4 tablespoons of the oil in a pan over a medium heat. Fry the aubergine (eggplant) slices for about 4 minutes on each side, until golden. Remove with a slotted spoon and drain on paper towels.

2 Meanwhile, cook the pasta as described on page 11. Return the drained pasta to the pan. Cover and keep warm.

3 Melt the butter in a small pan, stir in the flour and cook for 1 minute. Gradually pour in the milk, stirring all the time, then stir in the cream and chicken stock. Season with nutmeg, salt and pepper, bring to the boil and simmer for 5 minutes. Stir in the Cheddar and remove the pan from the heat. Pour half the sauce over the pasta and mix well. Reserve the remaining sauce.

4 Grease a shallow ovenproof dish. Spoon in half the pasta, cover it with half the lamb sauce and then with the aubergines (eggplant)

in a single layer. Repeat the
layers of pasta and lamb
sauce and spread the
remaining cheese sauce over
the top of the final layer.
Sprinkle with the Parmesan
and bake in a preheated
oven, 190°C/375°F/Gas
Mark 5, for 25 minutes, until
golden. Serve hot or cold,
with artichoke heart and
tomato salad.

Pasticcio

**A recipe with both Italian and Greek
origins, this dish may be served hot or cold.**

SERVES 6

250 g/8 oz fusilli, or other short pasta shapes
1 tbsp olive oil • 4 tbsp double (heavy) cream
salt • sprigs of rosemary to garnish

Sauce:
2 tbsp olive oil, plus extra for brushing • 1 onion, sliced thinly
1 red (bell) pepper, cored, deseeded and chopped
2 garlic cloves, chopped
625 g/1¼ lb minced (ground) lean beef
400 g/14 oz can of chopped tomatoes
120 ml/4 fl oz/½ cup dry white wine
2 tbsp chopped fresh parsley
60 g/2 oz can of anchovies, drained and chopped
salt and pepper

Topping:
300 ml/½ pint/1¼ cups natural yogurt • 3 eggs
pinch of freshly grated nutmeg
45 g/1½ oz/½ cup Parmesan, grated • salt and pepper

1 To make the sauce, heat the oil in a large frying pan (skillet) and fry the onion and (bell) pepper for 3 minutes. Stir in the garlic and cook for 1 minute. Stir in the beef and cook, stirring frequently, until it is no longer pink. Add the tomatoes and wine, stir well and bring to the boil.

Simmer, uncovered, for 20 minutes, until the sauce is fairly thick. Stir in the parsley and anchovies, and season to taste.

2 Cook the pasta as described on page 11. Transfer the drained pasta to a bowl. Stir in the cream and set aside.

3 To make the topping, beat together the yogurt and eggs and season with nutmeg, and salt and pepper. Stir in the cheese.

4 Brush a shallow baking dish with oil. Spoon in half the pasta and cover with half the meat sauce. Repeat these layers, spread the topping evenly and sprinkle on the cheese. Bake in a preheated oven, 190°C/ 375°F/Gas Mark 5, for 25 minutes, until the topping is golden brown and bubbling. Garnish with rosemary sprigs and serve with a selection of vegetable crudités.

Lasagne Verde

The sauce in this delicious baked pasta dish is the same sauce that is served with Spaghetti Bolognese (page 64).

SERVES 6

Ragù (page 64) • 1 tbsp olive oil
250 g/8 oz lasagne verde
60 g/2 oz/¾ cup Parmesan, grated
Béchamel Sauce (page 10) • salt and pepper
green salad, tomato salad or black olives, to serve

1 Begin by making the ragù as described on page 64. Cook for 10–12 minutes longer than the time given in an uncovered pan to reduce the sauce to the consistency of a thick paste.

2 Have ready a large pan of boiling, salted water and add the olive oil. Drop the pasta sheets into the boiling water a few at a time, and return the water to the boil before adding more pasta sheets. If you are using fresh lasagne, cook the sheets for 8 minutes. Cook dried or partly precooked pasta according to the directions on the packet. Remove the pasta sheets from the pan with a slotted spoon. Spread them in a single layer on damp tea towels.

3 Grease a rectangular ovenproof dish, about 25–28 cm/10–11 inches long. To assemble the lasagne verde, spoon a little of the ragù into the prepared dish, cover with a layer of lasagne, then spoon over a little béchamel sauce and sprinkle over some of the cheese. Continue making layers in this way, covering the final layer of lasagne with the remaining béchamel sauce.

4 Sprinkle on the remaining cheese and bake in a preheated oven, 190°C/375°F/Gas Mark 5, for 40 minutes, until the sauce is golden brown and bubbling. Serve with a green salad, a tomato salad, or a bowl of black olives.

Tex-Mex Ribs

The best ribs are those from the Jacob's Ladder, between the 1st and 5th rib.

SERVES 4–6

250 ml/ 8 fl oz/ 1 cup tomato ketchup
50 ml/ 2 fl oz/ ¼ cup cider vinegar
60 g/ 2 oz/ ⅓ cup light muscovado sugar
1 onion, chopped • 3 garlic cloves, crushed
1 tbsp dried chilli flakes • 2 tbsp Dijon mustard
1 tsp Worcestershire sauce • 2 kg/ 4 lb beef ribs

To serve:
1 French baguette, sliced • 125 g/ 4 oz/ ½ cup butter
3 garlic cloves, crushed • 1 tbsp chopped fresh parsley
1 avocado • lemon juice
250 g/ 8 oz mixed salad leaves (greens) • salt and pepper

1 Combine the ketchup, vinegar, sugar, onion, garlic, chilli flakes, mustard and Worcestershire sauce in a saucepan. Bring to the boil, and simmer for 10 minutes.

2 Wrap the ribs in foil, either in one piece or 3–4 smaller parcels. Cook over a medium-hot barbecue for 10 minutes, turning once or twice.

3 Meanwhile, combine the butter, garlic and parsley with plenty of salt and pepper. Spread the butter between each slice of the baguette and wrap in foil.

4 Peel and dice the avocado. Sprinkle over the lemon juice and mix together with the salad leaves.

5 Unwrap the ribs and place over the hot barbecue. Baste with the ketchup mixture. Cook for 20 minutes, turning occasionally. Meanwhile, cook the garlic bread for 15–20 minutes. Serve the ribs hot, with any leftover sauce for dipping, the garlic bread and the salad.

Vitello Tonnato

**Veal dishes are the speciality of Lombardy,
this being one of the more sophisticated.
Serve cold with seasonal salads.**

SERVES 4

*750 g/ 1½ lb boned leg of veal, rolled • 2 bay leaves
10 black peppercorns • 2–3 cloves
½ tsp salt • 2 carrots, sliced
1 onion, sliced • 2 celery stalks, sliced
about 750 ml/ 1¼ pints/ 3 cups stock or water
150 ml/ ¼ pint/ ²⁄₃ cup dry white wine (optional)*

Tuna sauce:

*90 g/ 3 oz canned tuna fish, well drained
50 g/ 1½ oz can of anchovy fillets, drained
150 ml/ ¼ pint/ ²⁄₃ cup olive oil
2 tsp bottled capers, drained • 2 egg yolks
1 tbsp lemon juice • salt and pepper*

To garnish:

lemon wedges • fresh herbs

1 Put the veal in a saucepan with the bay leaves, peppercorns, cloves, salt and vegetables. Add sufficient stock or water and the wine (if using) to barely cover the veal. Bring to the boil, remove any scum from the surface, then cover the pan and simmer gently for about 1 hour or until tender. Leave in the water until cold, then drain thoroughly. If time allows, chill the veal to make it easier to carve.

2 For the tuna sauce: thoroughly mash the tuna with 4 anchovy fillets, 1 tablespoon oil and the capers. Add the egg yolks and press through a sieve (strainer) or purée in a food processor or liquidizer until smooth. Stir in the lemon juice then gradually whisk in the rest of

the oil a few drops at a time until the sauce is smooth and has the consistency of thick cream. Season with salt and pepper to taste.

3 Slice the veal thinly and arrange on a serving platter. Spoon the sauce over the veal, then cover the dish and chill overnight. Before serving, uncover the veal. Decorate with the remaining anchovy fillets and the capers, and garnish with lemon wedges and herbs.

Sweet & Sour Pork Ribs

This recipe uses the spare rib, the traditional Chinese-style rib. However, baby back ribs and loin ribs are also suitable.

SERVES 4–6

2 garlic cloves, crushed
5 cm/2 inch piece of ginger, grated
150 ml/¼ pint/⅔ cup soy sauce
2 tbsp sugar
4 tbsp sweet sherry
4 tbsp tomato purée (paste)
300 g/10 oz/2 cups pineapple, cubed
2 kg/4 lb pork spare ribs
3 tbsp clear honey
5 pineapple rings, fresh or canned

1 Combine the garlic, ginger, soy sauce, sugar, sherry, tomato purée (paste) and cubed pineapple in a non-porous dish.

2 Put the spare ribs into the dish and make sure that they are coated completely with the marinade. Cover the dish and leave to marinate at room temperature for 2 hours only.

3 Cook the ribs over a medium-hot barbecue for 30–40 minutes, brushing with the honey after 20–30 minutes. Baste with the remaining marinade frequently until cooked completely.

4 Cook the pineapple rings over the barbecue for 10 minutes, turning once.

5 Serve the ribs with the pineapple rings on the side.

Sicilian Spaghetti

**This Sicilian dish originated as a handy
way of using up leftover cooked pasta.**

SERVES 4

*2 aubergines (eggplant), about 650 g/ 1½ lb
150 ml/¼ pint/⅔ cup olive oil
350 g/ 12 oz finely minced (ground) lean beef
1 onion, chopped • 2 garlic cloves, crushed
2 tbsp tomato purée (paste)
400 g/ 14 oz can of chopped tomatoes
1 tsp Worcestershire sauce
1 tsp chopped fresh oregano or marjoram or ½ tsp dried
oregano or marjoram
45 g/ 1½ oz pitted black olives, sliced
1 green, red or yellow (bell) pepper, cored, deseeded and chopped
175 g/ 6 oz spaghetti
125 g/ 4 oz/ 1¾ cups Parmesan, grated • salt and pepper
fresh oregano or parsley, to garnish (optional)*

1 Brush a 20 cm/8 inch loose-based round cake tin with oil, place a disc of baking parchment in the base and brush with oil.

2 Trim the aubergines (eggplant) and cut into slanting slices, 5 mm/¼ inch thick. Heat some of the oil in a frying pan (skillet). Fry a few slices at a time until lightly browned, turning once, and adding more oil as necessary. Drain on paper towels.

3 Put the minced (ground) beef, onion and garlic into a pan and cook until browned. Add the tomato purée (paste), tomatoes, Worcestershire sauce, herbs and seasoning. Simmer for 10 minutes, stirring. Add the olives and (bell) pepper and cook for 10 minutes.

4 Bring a large pan of salted water to the boil. Cook the spaghetti for 12–14 minutes until just tender. Drain. Turn the

spaghetti, the meat sauce and Parmesan into a bowl and mix, tossing with two forks.

5 Lay overlapping slices of aubergine (eggplant) evenly over the base of the cake tin and up the sides. Add the spaghetti mixture, pressing it down, and cover with the remaining slices of aubergine (eggplant).

6 Place in a roasting tin (pan) and cook in a preheated oven, 200°C/ 400°F/Gas Mark 6, for 40 minutes. Leave to stand for 5 minutes then loosen around the edges and invert on to a warmed serving dish, releasing the tin clip. Remove the paper. Sprinkle with herbs before serving, if using. Serve with extra Parmesan, if liked.

Kleftiko

**This classic Greek dish is usually made
with leg of lamb. Keep an eye on the
barbecue to ensure the heat remains
even during cooking.**

SERVES 6–8

1 kg/ 2 lb leg of lamb, boned and butterflied
5 garlic cloves, sliced
2 large rosemary sprigs, broken into 20 short lengths
6 tbsp olive oil • 4 tbsp lemon juice
2 tbsp chopped fresh mint • ½ tsp pepper
2 aubergines (eggplants), sliced lengthways

Rice pilau:
½ onion, chopped • 2 tbsp extra virgin olive oil
175 g/ 6 oz/ ¾ cup basmati rice
300 ml/ ½ pint/ 1¼ cups chicken stock • salt and pepper
1 tbsp pine kernels (nuts) • 1 tbsp chopped fresh oregano

1 Roll the lamb into a leg shape. Tuck in the shank (thin) end and fasten in place with skewers, preferably metal. Make 20 small nicks in the skin of the lamb with a knife. Insert a garlic slice and rosemary sprig into each nick.

2 Combine 4 tbsp of the olive oil with lemon juice, mint and pepper in a saucepan. Bring to a boil. Pour the simmering marinade over the lamb and rub in. Place the lamb on a piece of double foil or in a large foil tray on the grid over a medium-hot barbecue. Cook the lamb for 15 minutes, turning frequently. Then turn every 10–15 minutes for about 1 hour, until the lamb is cooked through. You may need to change the foil during this time to avoid flare-ups. The shank end will be more well cooked than the larger end.

3 Make the rice pilau. Heat the olive oil in a saucepan,

add the onion and fry over a
gentle heat until softened,
about 5 minutes. Add the rice
and stir until translucent. Add
the stock and bring to the boil.
Season well and simmer over
a gentle heat for 15 minutes.
Stir in the pine kernels (nuts)
and oregano. Keep warm.

4 Cut a lattice pattern in the
aubergine (eggplant) slices.
Brush with olive oil and cook
on the grid of the barbecue
for 10 minutes, turning once.

5 Slice the lamb and serve
with the aubergine
(eggplant) and rice pilau.

Pot Roasted Leg of Lamb

This dish from the Abruzzi uses a slow cooking method which ensures that the meat absorbs the flavourings and becomes very tender.

SERVES 4

1.75 kg/3½ lb leg of lamb • 3–4 sprigs of fresh rosemary
125 g/4 oz streaky bacon rashers • 4 tbsp olive oil
2–3 garlic cloves, crushed • 2 onions, sliced
2 carrots, sliced • 2 celery stalks, sliced
300 ml/½ pint/1¼ cups dry white wine
1 tbsp tomato purée (paste)
300 ml/½ pint/1¼ cups stock
350 g/12 oz tomatoes, peeled, quartered and deseeded
1 tbsp chopped fresh parsley
1 tbsp chopped fresh oregano or marjoram
salt and pepper • fresh rosemary sprigs, to garnish

1 Wipe the joint of lamb all over, trimming off any excess fat, then season well with salt and pepper, rubbing well in. Lay the sprigs of rosemary over the lamb, cover evenly with the bacon rashers and tie in place with fine string. Heat the oil in a frying pan (skillet) and fry the lamb until browned all over, turning several times – about 10 minutes. Remove from the pan.

2 Transfer the oil from the frying pan (skillet) to a large fireproof casserole and fry the garlic and onion together for 3–4 minutes until just beginning to soften. Add the carrots and celery, and continue to cook for a few minutes longer.

3 Lay the lamb on top of the vegetables and press well to partly submerge. Pour the wine over the lamb, add the tomato purée (paste) and simmer for 3–4 minutes. Add the stock, tomatoes, herbs and seasoning and bring back to the boil for 3–4 minutes.

4 Cover the casserole tightly and cook in a preheated oven, 180°C/350°F/Gas Mark 4, for 2–2¹/₂ hours, until very tender.

5 Remove the lamb from the casserole and if liked,

remove the bacon and herbs with the string. Keep warm. Strain the juices, skimming off any excess fat, and serve in a jug. Serve the vegetables around the joint or in a serving dish. Garnish with the rosemary.

Saltimbocca

Literally translated saltimbocca means 'jump into the mouth', and this quick, tasty veal dish almost does that.

SERVES 4

4 thin veal escalopes • 8 fresh sage leaves
4 thin slices prosciutto or Parma ham (same size as the veal)
flour, for dredging • 2 tbsp olive oil
30 g/ 1 oz/ 2 tbsp butter • 4 tbsp white wine
4 tbsp chicken stock • 4 tbsp Marsala
salt and pepper • fresh sage leaves, to garnish

1 Either leave the escalopes as they are or cut in half. Place the pieces on to a sheet of cling film (plastic wrap) or baking parchment, keeping well apart, and cover with another sheet. Using a meat mallet or rolling pin beat the escalopes gently until at least double in size and very thin.

2 Lightly season the veal with salt and pepper and lay two fresh sage leaves on the larger slices, or one on the smaller slices. Lay the prosciutto slices evenly over the escalopes to cover the sage and fit the size of the veal almost exactly. Secure the prosciutto to the veal with wooden cocktail sticks. If preferred, the large slices can be folded in half first. Dredge lightly with a little flour.

3 Heat the oil and butter in a large frying pan (skillet) and fry the escalopes until golden brown on each side and just cooked through – about 4 minutes for single slices or 5–6 minutes for folded slices. Take care not to overcook. Transfer to a serving dish and keep warm.

4 Add the wine, stock and Marsala to the pan and bring to the boil, stirring well to loosen all the sediment. Boil until reduced by almost half. Adjust the seasoning and pour the liquid over the saltimbocca. Serve at once, garnished with sage leaves.

Pizzaiola Steak

The Neapolitan sauce uses the delicious red tomatoes so abundant in that area, but canned ones make an excellent alternative.

SERVES 4

2 x 400 g/14 oz cans peeled tomatoes or
750 g/1½ lb fresh tomatoes
4 tbsp olive oil
2–3 garlic cloves, crushed • 1 onion, chopped finely
1 tbsp tomato purée (paste)
1½ tsp chopped fresh marjoram or oregano or
¾ tsp dried marjoram or oregano
4 thin sirloin or rump steaks • 2 tbsp chopped fresh parsley
1 tsp sugar • salt and pepper
fresh herbs, to garnish (optional)
sauté potatoes, to serve

1 If using canned tomatoes, purée them in a food processor, then sieve (strain) to remove the seeds. If using fresh tomatoes, peel, deseed and chop finely.

2 Heat half the oil in a pan and fry the garlic and onions very gently until soft – about 5 minutes. Add the tomatoes, seasoning, tomato purée (paste) and chopped herbs to the pan. If using fresh tomatoes add 4 tablespoons water, and then simmer very gently for 8–10 minutes, stirring occasionally.

3 Meanwhile, trim the steaks if necessary and season with salt and pepper. Heat the remaining oil in a frying pan and fry the steaks quickly on both sides to seal, then continue until cooked to your liking – 2 minutes for rare, 3–4 minutes for medium, or 5 minutes for well done. Alternatively, cook the steaks under a hot grill (broiler) after brushing lightly with oil.

4 When the sauce has thickened a little, adjust the seasoning and stir in the chopped parsley and sugar.

5 Pour off the excess fat from the pan containing the steaks and add the tomato sauce. Reheat gently and serve at once, with the sauce spooned over and around the steaks. Garnish with fresh herbs, if liked. Sauté potatoes make a good accompaniment with a green vegetable.

Fish & Seafood

Naturally low in fat, yet rich in
minerals and proteins, white fish
and shellfish will be important
ingredients in a low-fat diet. After
pasta, fish is probably the most
popular food in Italy, and in
many of these recipes you will
find these two ingredients
combined to great effect.

Salmon Fillet on a
Bed of Herbs

**This is a great party dish, as the salmon is
cooked in one piece. Even though it is
cooked on a layer of herbs, it manages to
keep a smoky, barbecued flavour.**

SERVES 4

½ large bunch dried thyme
5 fresh rosemary branches, 15–20 cm/6–8 inches long
8 bay leaves
1 kg/2 lb salmon fillet
1 bulb fennel, cut into 8 pieces
2 tbsp lemon juice
2 tbsp olive oil

1 Make a base on a hot
barbecue with the dried
thyme, rosemary branches
and bay leaves, overlapping
them so that they cover a
slightly bigger area than the
salmon fillet.

2 Place the salmon on top
of the herbs.

3 Arrange the pieces of
fennel around the edge of
the salmon.

4 Combine the lemon juice
and oil and brush over
the salmon with it.

5 Cover the salmon loosely
with a piece of foil, to
keep it moist.

6 Cook the salmon for
about 20–30 minutes,
basting frequently with the
lemon juice mixture.

7 Remove the salmon from
the barbecue, cut it into
slices and serve with the
fennel pieces.

Spaghetti with Tuna & Parsley Sauce

This is a recipe to look forward to when parsley is at its most prolific, during the summer.

SERVES 4

500 g/1 lb 2 oz spaghetti
1 tbsp olive oil
30 g/1 oz/2 tbsp butter
black olives, to garnish

Sauce:
200 g/7 oz can of tuna, drained
60 g/2 oz can of anchovies, drained
250 ml/8 fl oz/1 cup olive oil
60 g/2 oz/1 cup roughly chopped fresh, flat-leaf parsley
150 ml/¼ pint/²⁄₃ cup crème fraîche
salt and pepper

1 Cook the spaghetti as described on page 11. Return the drained pasta to the pan, add the butter, toss thoroughly to coat, cover and keep warm.

2 To make the sauce, remove any bones from the tuna. Put it into a blender or food processor with the anchovies, olive oil and parsley and process until the sauce is smooth. Pour in the crème fraîche and process for a few seconds to blend. Taste the sauce and season.

3 Warm 4 plates. Warm the pan of spaghetti over a medium heat, shaking, until it is heated through. Pour on the sauce and toss quickly, using 2 forks.

4 Transfer to the serving plates, garnish with the olives and serve hot.

Baked Sea Bass

**Sea bass is a delicious white-fleshed fish.
Two small fish are succulent grilled
(broiled), but a large fish is best baked.**

SERVES 4

*1.5 kg/3 lb fresh sea bass or
2 × 750 g/1½ lb sea bass, gutted
2–4 sprigs fresh rosemary • ½ lemon, sliced thinly
2 tbsp olive oil*

Garlic sauce:

*2 tsp coarse sea salt • 2 tsp capers
2 garlic cloves, crushed • 4 tbsp water
2 fresh bay leaves • 1 tsp lemon juice or wine vinegar
2 tbsp olive oil • pepper*

To garnish:

bay leaves • lemon wedges

1 Scrape off the scales from the fish and cut off the sharp fins. Make diagonal cuts along both sides. Wash and dry thoroughly. Place a sprig of rosemary in the cavity of each of the smaller fish with half the lemon slices; or two sprigs and all the lemon in the large fish.

2 To grill (broil): place in a foil-lined pan (tin), brush lightly with 1–2 tablespoons of oil and grill (broil) under a moderate heat for about 5 minutes on each side or until cooked through, turning carefully.

3 To bake: place the fish in a foil-lined dish or roasting tin (pan) brushed with oil, and brush the fish with the rest of the oil. Cook in a preheated oven, 190°C/375°F/Gas Mark 5 for about 30 minutes for the small fish or 45–50 minutes for the large fish, until the thickest part of the fish is opaque.

4 For the sauce: crush the salt and capers with the garlic in a pestle and mortar and then gradually work in the water. Alternatively, put the ingredients into a food processor or blender and blend until smooth. Bruise the bay leaves and the remaining sprigs of rosemary and put in a bowl. Add the garlic mixture, lemon juice or vinegar and oil and pound together. Season with pepper.

5 Place the fish on a warmed serving dish and, if liked, carefully remove the skin. Spoon some sauce over the fish and serve the rest separately. Garnish with bay leaves and lemon wedges.

Sardine & Potato Bake

Fresh sardines are now readily available, so this dish from Liguria can be enjoyed by all.

SERVES 4

1 kg/ 2 lb potatoes
1 kg/ 2 lb sardines, defrosted if frozen
1 tbsp olive oil, plus extra for oiling • 1 onion, chopped
2–3 garlic cloves, crushed • 2 tbsp chopped fresh parsley
350 g/ 12 oz ripe tomatoes, peeled and sliced
or 400 g/ 14 oz can of peeled tomatoes, partly
drained and chopped
1–2 tbsp chopped fresh Italian herbs, such as oregano, thyme,
rosemary, marjoram
150 ml/ ¼ pint/ ⅔ cup dry white wine • salt and pepper

1 Put the potatoes in a pan of salted water, bring to the boil, cover and simmer for 10 minutes then drain. When cool enough to handle, cut into slices about 5 mm/ ¼ inch thick.

2 Gut and clean the fish, cut off their heads and tails, and slit open the length of the belly. Turn the fish over so the skin is upwards and press firmly along the backbone to loosen the bones. Turn over again and carefully remove the backbone. Wash the fish in cold water, drain well and dry on paper towels.

3 Heat the oil in a pan and fry the onion and garlic until soft, but not coloured. Arrange the potatoes in a well-oiled ovenproof dish and sprinkle with the onions and then the parsley and plenty of seasoning. Lay the open sardines over the potatoes, skin-side down, then cover with the tomatoes and the Italian herbs. Pour on the wine and season again.

4 Cook uncovered in a preheated oven, 190°C/ 375°F/Gas Mark 5, for about 40 minutes until the fish is tender. If the casserole dries out, add more wine.

Spaghetti with Seafood

**Frozen shelled prawns (shrimp) can be
used in this colourful and tasty dish.**

SERVES 4

*250 g/ 8 oz short-cut spaghetti, or long spaghetti broken into
15 cm/ 6 inch lengths
2 tbsp olive oil • 300 ml/½ pint/ 1¼ cups chicken stock
1 tsp lemon juice • 1 small cauliflower, cut into florets
2 carrots, sliced thinly
125 g/ 4 oz mangetout (snow peas), trimmed
60 g/ 2 oz/ 4 tbsp butter • 1 onion, sliced
250 g/ 8 oz courgettes (zucchini), sliced thinly
1 garlic clove, chopped
350 g/ 12 oz frozen shelled prawns (shrimp), defrosted
2 tbsp chopped fresh parsley
30 g/ 1 oz/ ¼ cup Parmesan, grated
½ tsp paprika • salt and pepper
4 unshelled prawns (shrimp), to garnish (optional)*

1 Cook the pasta as
described on page 11.
Return the drained pasta to
the pan and stir in the
remaining olive oil. Cover
and keep warm.

2 Bring the chicken stock
and lemon juice to the
boil. Add the cauliflower and
carrots and cook for 3–4
minutes until they are just
tender. Remove with a slotted
spoon and set aside. Add the
mangetout (snow peas) and
cook for 1–2 minutes, until

they begin to soften. Remove
with a slotted spoon and add
to the carrots. Reserve the
stock for future use.

3 Melt half the butter in
a frying pan (skillet) over
a medium heat and fry the
onion and courgettes
(zucchini) for about 3
minutes. Add the garlic and
prawns (shrimp) and cook for
2–3 minutes until thoroughly
heated through. Stir in the
reserved vegetables and heat
through. Season with salt

and pepper then stir in the remaining butter.

4 Transfer the spaghetti to a warmed serving dish. Pour on the sauce and parsley. Toss well using 2 forks, until thoroughly coated. Sprinkle on the grated cheese and paprika, and garnish with unshelled prawns (shrimp), if using. Serve immediately.

Swordfish Steak with Roast Garlic

On a Saturday morning the fish market in Sydney is packed with people buying fish for their weekend 'barbies', and swordfish is a very popular choice.

SERVES 4

4 swordfish steaks, about 200 g/7 oz each
4 tbsp olive oil
2 whole garlic bulbs
pepper

1 Brush the swordfish steaks with the olive oil and season well. Set aside.

2 Cook the whole unpeeled garlic bulbs over a very hot barbecue for about 25 minutes until they are soft to the touch. It is difficult to overcook the garlic, but keep an eye on it nevertheless.

3 After the garlic has been cooking for about 15 minutes, put the steaks on the barbecue and cook for 5–6 minutes on each side, until the flesh is firm and flakes easily. Brush once or twice with the olive oil during cooking.

4 When the garlic is soft to the touch, cut across the top of it, exposing all the cloves.

5 When the swordfish steaks are cooked, place on a serving plate. Squeeze the garlic cloves out of their skins and rub all over liberally. Season with pepper and serve immediately.

Trout in Red Wine

**This recipe from Trentino is best when the
fish are freshly caught, but it gives any
trout an interesting flavour.**

SERVES 4

*4 fresh trout, about 300 g/ 10 oz each
250 ml/ 8 fl oz/ 1 cup red wine vinegar
300 ml/ ½ pint/ 1¼ cups red wine
150 ml/ ¼ pint/ ⅔ cup water
1 carrot, sliced • 2–4 bay leaves
thinly pared rind of 1 lemon
1 small onion, sliced very thinly • 4 sprigs of fresh parsley
4 sprigs of fresh thyme • 1 tsp black peppercorns
6–8 whole cloves • 90 g/ 3 oz/ 6 tbsp butter
1 tbsp chopped fresh mixed herbs • sea salt and pepper*

To garnish:
sprigs of herbs • lemon slices

1 Gut the trout but leave
the heads on. Dry on
paper towels and lay the fish
head to tail in a shallow
container or baking tin (pan)
just large enough to hold
them. Bring the wine vinegar
to the boil and pour slowly all
over the fish. Leave the fish
to marinate in the refrigerator
for 20 minutes.

2 Put the wine, water,
carrot, bay leaves, lemon
rind, onion, herbs, peppercorns and cloves into a pan
with a good pinch of sea salt
and heat gently.

3 Drain the fish thoroughly,
discarding the vinegar.
Place the fish in a fish kettle
or large frying pan (skillet) so
they touch. When the wine
mixture boils, strain gently
over the fish so they are
about half covered. Cover the
pan and simmer very gently
for 15 minutes.

4 Carefully remove the fish
from the pan, draining off

as much of the liquid as possible, and arrange on a serving dish. Keep warm.

5 Boil the cooking liquid until reduced to about 4–6 tablespoons. Melt the butter in a small saucepan and strain in the cooking liquor. Adjust the seasoning and spoon over the fish. Sprinkle with chopped mixed herbs and garnish with fresh herbs and lemon slices.

Steamed Pasta Pudding

**A tasty mixture of creamy fish and
macaroni cooked in a bowl.**

SERVES 4

*125 g/4 oz short-cut macaroni, or other short pasta shapes
1 tbsp olive oil
15 g/½ oz/1 tbsp butter, plus extra for greasing
500 g/1 lb 2 oz white fish fillets, such as cod, haddock or coley
a few parsley stalks • 6 black peppercorns
120 ml/4 fl oz/½ cup double (heavy) cream
2 eggs, separated • 2 tbsp chopped fresh dill, or parsley
freshly ground black pepper • freshly grated nutmeg
60 g/2 oz/¾ cup Parmesan, grated
Tomato Sauce (page 10), to serve
dill or parsley sprigs, to garnish*

1 Cook the pasta as described on page 11. Return the drained pasta to the pan, add the butter and cover the pan. Keep warm.

2 Place the fish in a frying pan (skillet) with the parsley stalks, peppercorns and just enough water to cover. Bring to the boil, cover, and simmer for 10 minutes. Lift out the fish with a fish slice, reserving the liquor. When the fish is cool enough to handle, skin and remove any remaining bones. Cut into bite-sized pieces.

3 Transfer the pasta to a large bowl and stir in the cream, egg yolks, dill and pepper. Stir in the fish and enough liquor to make the mixture moist but firm; it should fall easily from a spoon but not be too runny. Whisk the egg whites until stiff, then fold into the mixture.

4 Grease a heatproof bowl or pudding basin and spoon in the mixture to within 4 cm/1½ inches of the rim. Cover the top with greased baking parchment and a cloth, or with foil, and tie firmly around the rim.

5 Stand the pudding on a trivet in a large pan of boiling water to come halfway up the sides. Cover and steam for 1½ hours, topping up the boiling water as needed.

6 Run a knife around the inside of the bowl and invert on to a warmed serving dish. Pour tomato sauce over the top and garnish with the herb sprigs. Serve the nutmeg and Parmesan separately.

Seafood Lasagne

·A delicious variation of a classic pasta dish.

SERVES 6

8 sheets wholewheat lasagne • 1 tbsp olive oil
500 g/ 1 lb 2 oz smoked cod • 600 ml/ 1 pint/ 2½ cups milk
1 tbsp lemon juice • 8 peppercorns
2 bay leaves • a few parsley stalks
60 g/ 2 oz/ ¾ cup mature (sharp) Cheddar, grated
30 g/ 1 oz/ ½ cup Parmesan, grated
a few whole prawns (shrimp), to garnish (optional)

Sauce:

60 g/ 2 oz/ ¼ cup butter, plus extra for greasing
1 large onion, sliced
1 green (bell) pepper, cored, deseeded and chopped
1 small courgette (zucchini), sliced • 60 g/ 2 oz/ ½ cup flour
150 ml/ ¼ pint/ ⅔ cup white wine
150 ml/ ¼ pint/ ⅔ cup single (light) cream
125 g/ 4 oz shelled prawns (shrimp)
60 g/ 2 oz/ ½ cup mature (sharp) Cheddar, grated
salt and pepper

1 Cook the lasagne as described on page 116.

2 Place the cod, milk, lemon juice, peppercorns, bay leaves and parsley stalks in a frying pan (skillet). Bring to the boil, cover and simmer for 10 minutes. Lift the fish out with a slotted spoon. Remove the skin and bones and flake the fish with a fork. Strain and reserve the liquor.

3 Make the sauce: melt the butter in a pan and cook the onion, (bell) pepper and courgette (zucchini) for 2–3 minutes. Stir in the flour and cook for 1 minute. Stir in the fish liquor, wine, cream and prawns (shrimp), and simmer for 2 minutes. Remove from heat, add cheese, and season.

4 Grease a shallow baking dish. Pour in a quarter of

the sauce and spread evenly over the base. Cover the sauce with 3 sheets of lasagne, then with another quarter of the sauce. Arrange the fish on top, then cover with half the remaining sauce. Finish with the remaining lasagne, then the rest of the sauce. Sprinkle the Cheddar and Parmesan over the sauce.

5 Bake in a preheated oven, 190°C/375°F/ Gas Mark 5, for 25 minutes, or until the top is golden brown and bubbling. Garnish with a few whole prawns (shrimp), if liked.

Sea Bass Baked in Foil

Sea bass is often paired with subtle oriental flavours. For a special occasion, you may like to bone the fish, so that your guests can cut straight through the flesh.

SERVES 4–6

2 sea bass, about 1 kg/2 lb each, gutted and scaled
2 spring onions (scallions), green part only, cut into strips
5 cm/2 inch piece of ginger, peeled and cut into strips
2 garlic cloves, unpeeled, crushed lightly
2 tbsp mirin or dry sherry
salt and pepper

To serve:
pickled sushi ginger (optional)
soy sauce

1 For each fish lay out a double thickness of foil. Oil the top piece of foil well, or lay a piece of silicon paper over the foil. Place the fish in the middle and expose the cavity.

2 Divide the spring onions (scallions) and ginger between each cavity. Put a garlic clove in each cavity. Pour over the mirin or dry sherry. Season the fish well.

3 Close the cavities and lay each fish on its side. Fold over the foil and seal the edges together securely. Fold each end neatly.

4 Cook the fish over a medium-hot barbecue for 15 minutes, turning once.

5 To serve, remove the foil and cut each fish into 2 or 3 pieces. Serve with the pickled ginger, if using, accompanied by soy sauce.

Italian Fish Stew

This wonderfully robust stew is full of fine Mediterranean flavours such as basil, lemon and tomato. As you can use any firm white fish, it's ideal for using whatever is most economical.

SERVES 4

2 tbsp olive oil • 2 red onions, finely chopped
1 garlic clove, crushed
2 courgettes (zucchini), sliced
400 g/ 14 oz can of chopped tomatoes
900 ml/ 1½ pints/ 3½ cups fish or vegetable stock
90 g/ 3 oz dried pasta shapes
350 g/ 12 oz firm white fish, such as cod, haddock or hake
1 tbsp chopped fresh basil or oregano or 1 tsp dried oregano
1 tsp grated lemon rind
1 tbsp cornflour (cornstarch)
1 tbsp water • salt and pepper
sprigs of fresh basil or oregano, to garnish

1 Heat the oil in a large saucepan and fry the onions and garlic for 5 minutes. Add the courgettes (zucchini) and cook for 2–3 minutes, stirring often. Add the tomatoes and stock to the saucepan and bring to the boil. Add the pasta, cover and reduce the heat. Simmer for 5 minutes.

2 Skin and bone the fish, then cut into chunks. Add to the saucepan with the basil or oregano and lemon rind and cook gently for 5 minutes until the fish is opaque and flakes easily. Take care not to overcook it.

3 Blend the cornflour (cornstarch) with the water and stir into the stew. Cook gently for 2 minutes, stirring, until thickened. Season to taste and ladle into 4 warmed soup bowls. Garnish with basil or oregano sprigs and serve at once.

Spaghetti with Smoked Salmon

Made in moments, this is a dish to impress and delight unexpected guests.

SERVES 4

500 g/1 lb 2 oz buckwheat spaghetti
2 tbsp olive oil
90 g/3 oz/½ cup Feta cheese, crumbled
coriander (cilantro) or parsley, to garnish

Sauce:
300 ml/½ pint/1¼ cups double (heavy) cream
150 ml/¼ pint/⅔ cup whisky or brandy
125 g/4 oz smoked salmon
large pinch of cayenne pepper
2 tbsp chopped fresh coriander (cilantro) or parsley
salt and pepper

1 Cook the pasta as described on page 11. Return the drained pasta to the pan and sprinkle on the remaining oil. Cover and shake the pan, then set aside and keep warm.

2 In separate small pans, heat the cream and the whisky or brandy to simmering point. Do not let them boil.

3 Combine the cream with the whisky or brandy. Cut the smoked salmon into thin strips and add to the cream mixture. Season with pepper and cayenne, and stir in the coriander (cilantro) or parsley.

4 Transfer the spaghetti to a warmed serving dish, pour on the sauce and toss thoroughly using 2 large forks. Scatter the Feta cheese over the pasta and garnish with the coriander (cilantro) or parsley. Serve hot.

Macaroni & Prawn (Shrimp) Bake

This adaptation of an 18th-century Italian dish is served cut into wedges, like a cake.

SERVES 4

350 g/12 oz short pasta, such as short-cut macaroni
1 tbsp olive oil, plus extra for brushing
90 g/3 oz/6 tbsp butter, plus extra for greasing
2 small fennel bulbs, sliced thinly, leaves reserved
175 g/6 oz mushrooms, sliced thinly
175 g/6 oz shelled prawns (shrimp)
Béchamel Sauce (page 10) • pinch of cayenne pepper
60 g/2 oz/¾ cup Parmesan, grated • 2 tomatoes, sliced
1 tsp dried oregano • salt and pepper

1 Cook the pasta as described on page 11. Return the drained pasta to the saucepan and dot with 30 g/1 oz/2 tablespoons of the butter. Shake the pan well, cover and keep warm.

2 Melt the remaining butter in a pan over a medium heat and fry the fennel for 3–4 minutes, until it begins to soften. Stir in the mushrooms and fry for a further 2 minutes. Stir in the prawns (shrimp), remove the pan from the heat and set aside, covered.

3 Make the béchamel sauce and add the cayenne pepper. Remove the pan from the heat and stir in the reserved vegetables, prawns (shrimp) and the pasta. Grease a round, shallow baking dish. Pour in the pasta mixture and spread evenly. Sprinkle on the Parmesan, and arrange the tomato slices in a ring on top. Brush the tomato with oil and sprinkle on the dried oregano.

4 Bake in a preheated oven, 180°C/350°F/Gas Mark 4, for 25 minutes, until golden brown. Serve hot.

Scallop Skewers

Frozen scallops are fine to use for this recipe. Serve with a rocket (arugula) salad to emphasize the Californian origin of the dish.

SERVES 4

grated zest and juice of 2 limes
2 tbsp finely chopped lemon grass or 1 tbsp lemon juice
2 garlic cloves, crushed
1 green chilli, deseeded and chopped
16 scallops, with corals • 2 limes, each cut into 8 segments
2 tbsp sunflower oil • 1 tbsp lemon juice
salt and pepper

To serve:
60 g/2 oz/1 cup rocket (arugula) salad
200 g/7 oz/3 cups mixed salad leaves (greens)

1 Soak 8 wooden skewers in warm water for at least 20 minutes before using them.

2 Meanwhile, combine the lime zest and juice, lemon grass or lemon juice, garlic and chilli together in a pestle and mortar or spice grinder to make a paste.

3 Whisk together the oil, lemon juice, salt and pepper thoroughly to make the salad dressing.

4 Thread 2 scallops on to each of the soaked skewers, alternating with 2 lime segments.

5 Coat the scallops with the spice paste and place over a medium-hot barbecue, basting occasionally. Cook for 10 minutes, turning once.

6 Toss the rocket (arugula), mixed salad leaves (greens) and dressing together.

7 Serve the scallops piping hot, 2 skewers on each plate, with the rocket (arugula) and salad leaves (greens).

Pasta Shells with Mussels

An aromatic and garlicky seafood dish.

SERVES 4–6

400 g/14 oz pasta shells • 1 tbsp olive oil

Sauce:
3.5 litres/6 pints mussels, scrubbed
250 ml/8 fl oz/1 cup dry white wine
2 large onions, chopped
125 g/4 oz/½ cup unsalted butter
6 large garlic cloves, chopped finely
5 tbsp chopped fresh parsley
300 ml/½ pint/1¼ cups double (heavy) cream
salt and pepper • crusty bread, to serve

1 Pull off the 'beards' from the mussels and rinse well in several changes of water. Discard any that do not close when tapped. Put the mussels in a large pan with the white wine and half the onions. Cover the pan, shake and cook over a medium heat for 2–3 minutes until the mussels open. Remove from the heat, lift out the mussels with a slotted spoon, reserving the liquor, and set aside until they are cool enough to handle. Discard any mussels that have not opened.

2 Melt the butter in a pan over a medium heat and fry the remaining onion until translucent. Stir in the garlic and cook for 1 minute. Gradually pour on the reserved cooking liquor, stirring to blend well. Stir in the parsley and cream. Season and bring to simmering point.

3 Cook the pasta as described on page 11. Return the pasta to the pan, cover and keep warm.

4 Remove the mussels from their shells, reserving a few shells for garnish. Stir the mussels into the cream sauce. Tip the pasta into a warmed serving dish, pour on the

sauce and mix. Garnish
with a few mussel shells

and serve hot, with warm,
crusty bread.

Squid & Macaroni Stew

This seafood dish is quick and easy to make, yet is deliciously satisfying to eat.

SERVES 4–6

250 g/ 8 oz short-cut macaroni, or other short pasta shapes
1 tbsp olive oil • 2 tbsp chopped fresh parsley
salt and pepper • crusty bread, to serve

Sauce:
6 tbsp olive oil • 2 onions, sliced
350 g/ 12 oz cleaned squid, cut into 4 cm/ ½ inch strips
250 ml/ 8 fl oz/ 1 cup fish stock
150 ml/ ¼ pint/ ⅔ cup red wine
350 g/ 12 oz tomatoes, peeled and thinly sliced
2 tbsp tomato purée (paste) • 1 tsp dried oregano
2 bay leaves • salt and pepper

1 Cook the pasta for only 3 minutes in a pan of boiling salted water, adding the oil. Drain, return to the pan, cover and keep warm.

2 To make the sauce, heat the oil in a pan over medium heat and fry the onion until translucent. Add the squid and stock and simmer for 5 minutes. Pour on the wine and add the tomatoes, tomato purée (paste), oregano and bay leaves. Bring to the boil, season and cook, uncovered, for 5 minutes.

3 Add the pasta, stir well, cover the pan and simmer for 10 minutes, or until the squid and pasta are almost tender. The sauce should be syrupy; if it is too liquid, continue cooking, uncovered, for a few minutes. Adjust the seasoning if necessary.

4 Remove the bay leaves and stir in most of the parsley, reserving a little to garnish. Transfer to a warmed serving dish. Sprinkle on the remaining parsley and serve hot with warm, crusty bread such as ciabatta.

Baby Octopus & Squid with Chilli Sauce

This is a delicious and unusual recipe, best served with a simple green salad.

SERVES 4–6

150 ml/¼ pint/⅔ cup rice vinegar
50 ml/2 fl oz/¼ cup dry sherry
2 red chillies, deseeded and chopped • 1 tsp sugar • 4 tbsp oil
12 baby octopus • 12 small squid tubes, cleaned
2 spring onions (scallions), sliced • 1 garlic clove, crushed
2.5 cm/1 inch piece ginger, grated
4 tbsp sweet chilli sauce • salt

1 Combine the vinegar, sherry, chillies, sugar, 2 tbsp of the oil and a pinch of salt in a large bowl.

2 Wash each octopus under cold running water and drain. Lay each on its side on a chopping board. Remove the head and beak and discard. Put the tentacles, which should all be in one piece, into the vinegar mixture with the squid tubes. Cover and chill for 8 hours or overnight.

3 Put the remaining oil into a frying pan (skillet) or wok and add the spring onions (scallions), garlic and ginger. Stir for 1 minute over a very hot barbecue. Remove from the heat and add the chilli sauce. Set aside.

4 Drain the fish from the marinade. Cut the pointed bottom end off each squid tube, so that you are left with tubes of even width all the way down. Make a cut down one side and open out the squid so that it is flat. Make four cuts in one direction and four in the other to create a lattice pattern.

5 Cook the octopus and squid over the hottest part of the barbecue for 4–5 minutes, turning constantly.

The octopus tentacles will curl up, and are cooked when the flesh is no longer translucent. The squid tubes will curl back on themselves, revealing the lattice cuts. When cooked, toss them into the pan with the chilli sauce to coat and serve immediately.

Vermicelli with Clam Sauce

A quickly cooked seafood dish with style.

SERVES 4

400 g/14 oz vermicelli, spaghetti, or other long pasta
1 tbsp olive oil • 30 g/1 oz/2 tbsp butter
2 tbsp Parmesan shavings, to garnish
sprig of basil, to garnish

Sauce:
1 tbsp olive oil • 2 onions, chopped
2 garlic cloves, chopped
2 × 200 g/7 oz jars of clams in brine
120 ml/4 fl oz/½ cup white wine
4 tbsp chopped fresh parsley • ½ tsp dried oregano
pinch of freshly grated nutmeg • salt and pepper

1 Cook the pasta as described on page 11. Return the drained pasta to the pan and add the butter. Cover and shake the pan, then set aside and keep warm.

2 To make the clam sauce, heat the oil in a pan over a medium heat and fry the onion until it is translucent. Stir in the garlic and cook for 1 minute. Strain the brine from 1 jar of clams, pour into the pan and add the wine. Stir well and simmer for 3 minutes. Drain the brine from the second jar of clams and discard.

3 Add the clams and herbs to the pan, and season with pepper and nutmeg. Lower the heat and cook until the sauce is heated through.

4 Transfer the pasta to a warmed serving dish and pour over the sauce. Sprinkle with the Parmesan shavings and garnish with the sprig of basil. Serve hot.

Squid Casserole

Squid is often served fried in Italy, but here it is casseroled with tomatoes and (bell) peppers to give a rich sauce.

SERVES 4

1 kg/2 lb whole squid, cleaned
or 750 g/1½ lb squid rings, defrosted if frozen
3 tbsp olive oil • 1 large onion, sliced thinly
2 garlic cloves, crushed
1 red (bell) pepper, cored, deseeded and sliced
1–2 sprigs fresh rosemary
150 ml/¼ pint/⅔ cup dry white wine and
250 ml/8 fl oz/1 cup water, or
350 ml/12 fl oz/1½ cups water or fish stock
400 g/14 oz can of chopped tomatoes
2 tbsp tomato purée (paste)
1 tsp paprika • salt and pepper
fresh sprigs of rosemary or parsley, to garnish

1 Cut the squid pouch into 1 cm/½ inch slices; cut the tentacles into 5 cm/2 inch lengths. Frozen squid rings should be fully defrosted and well drained.

2 Heat the oil in a flame-proof casserole and fry the onion and garlic until soft. Add the squid, increase the heat and cook for about 10 minutes until sealed and beginning to colour lightly. Add the red (bell) pepper, rosemary and wine (if using), and water or stock and bring to the boil. Cover and simmer gently for 45 minutes.

3 Discard the rosemary. Add the tomatoes, tomato purée (paste), seasonings and paprika. Continue to simmer gently for 45–60 minutes, or cover the casserole tightly and cook in the oven, 180°C/350°F/Gas Mark 4, for 45–60 minutes until tender. Give the sauce a good stir, adjust the seasoning and serve hot.

Vegetable Dishes

Anyone who ever thought that
vegetarian meals were dull will
think again when they see the
recipes in this chapter. There are
meals of many differing styles –
casseroles, pies, bakes, stir-fries,
rice and pasta dishes, displaying
influences from Thai, Mexican
and Italian cuisine.

Chilled Noodles & (Bell) Pepper Sauce

This is a convenient dish to serve when you are arriving home just before family or friends. You can have it all prepared and ready to assemble in minutes.

SERVES 4–6

250 g / 8 oz ribbon noodles, or Chinese egg noodles
1 tbsp sesame oil • 1 red (bell) pepper
1 yellow (bell) pepper • 1 green (bell) pepper
6 spring onions (scallions), cut into matchsticks • salt

Dressing:
5 tbsp sesame oil • 2 tbsp light soy sauce
1 tbsp tahini (sesame paste) • 4–5 drops hot pepper sauce

1 Preheat the grill (broiler) to medium. Cook the noodles in a large pan of boiling, salted water until they are almost tender. Drain in a colander, run cold water over them and drain again thoroughly. Tip the noodles into a bowl, stir in the sesame oil, cover and chill.

2 Cook the (bell) peppers under the grill (broiler), turning them frequently, until they are blackened on all sides. Plunge them into cold water, then skin them. Cut in half, remove the core and seeds and cut the flesh into thick strips. Set aside, covered.

3 To make the dressing, mix together the sesame oil, soy sauce, tahini (sesame paste) and hot pepper sauce.

4 Pour the dressing over the noodles, reserving 1 tablespoon, and toss well. Turn the noodles into a serving dish, arrange the (bell) pepper strips over the noodles and spoon on the reserved dressing. Scatter over the spring onion (scallion) strips.

Three-Cheese
Macaroni Bake

**Based on a traditional family favourite, this
pasta bake has plenty of flavour. Serve with
a crisp salad for a quick, tasty supper.**

SERVES 4

600 ml/1 pint/2½ cups béchamel sauce
250 g/8 oz/2 cups macaroni • 1 egg, beaten
125 g/4 oz/1¾ cups mature (sharp) Cheddar, grated
1 tbsp wholegrain mustard
2 tbsp chopped fresh chives
4 tomatoes, sliced
125 g/4 oz/1¾ cups Red Leicester (brick) cheese, grated
60 g/2 oz/¾ cup blue cheese, grated
2 tbsp sunflower seeds • salt and pepper
snipped fresh chives, to garnish

1 Make the béchamel sauce, put into a bowl and cover with cling film (plastic wrap) to prevent a skin forming. Set aside.

2 Bring a saucepan of salted water to the boil and cook the macaroni for 8–10 minutes until just tender. Drain well and place in an ovenproof dish.

3 Stir the beaten egg, Cheddar, mustard, chives and salt and pepper to taste into the béchamel sauce and spoon over the macaroni, making sure it is well covered. Top with a layer of sliced tomatoes.

4 Sprinkle over the Red Leicester (brick) and blue cheeses, and sunflower seeds. Place on a baking sheet (cookie sheet) and bake in a preheated oven, 190°C/ 375°F/Gas Mark 5, for 25–30 minutes until bubbling and golden. Garnish with chives and serve hot.

Mushroom & Nut Crumble

A tasty dish that is ideal for a warming family supper. The crunchy topping is flavoured with three different types of nuts.

SERVES 4

350 g/12 oz open-cup mushrooms, sliced
350 g/12 oz chestnut mushrooms, sliced
400 ml/14 fl oz/1¾ cups vegetable stock
60 g/2 oz/4 tbsp butter or margarine
1 large onion, chopped finely • 1 garlic clove, crushed
60 g/2 oz/½ cup plain (all-purpose) flour
4 tbsp double (heavy) cream
2 tbsp chopped fresh parsley
salt and pepper • fresh herbs, to garnish

Crumble topping:
90 g/3 oz/¾ cup medium oatmeal
90 g/3 oz/¾ cup wholemeal (whole wheat) flour
1 tsp dried thyme • 30 g/1 oz/¼ cup ground almonds
30 g/1 oz/¼ cup finely chopped walnuts
60 g/2 oz/½ cup finely chopped unsalted shelled pistachio nuts
90 g/3 oz/⅓ cup butter or margarine, softened
1 tbsp fennel seeds

1 Put the mushrooms and stock in a large saucepan, bring to the boil, cover and simmer for 15 minutes until tender. Drain thoroughly, reserving the stock.

2 In another saucepan, melt the butter or margarine, and gently fry the onion and garlic for 2–3 minutes until just softened but not browned. Stir in the flour and cook for 1 minute.

3 Remove the pan from the heat and gradually stir in the reserved mushroom stock. Return to the heat and cook, stirring, until thickened. Stir in the mushrooms, salt and pepper to taste, cream and

parsley and spoon into a
shallow ovenproof dish.

4 To make the topping, mix
together the oatmeal,
flour, thyme, nuts and salt and
pepper to taste. Using a fork,
mix in the butter or
margarine until the topping
resembles coarse breadcrumbs.

5 Sprinkle the topping over
the mushrooms, scatter
over the fennel seeds and
bake in a preheated oven,
190°C/375°F/Gas Mark 5,
for 25–30 minutes until
golden and crisp. Garnish
with herbs and serve hot.

Pasta with Green Vegetables

**The fresh vegetables make this a
mouthwateringly light summer dish.**

SERVES 4

250 g/ 8 oz gemelli or other pasta shapes
1 tbsp olive oil
2 tbsp chopped fresh parsley
2 tbsp freshly grated Parmesan

Sauce:
1 head green broccoli, cut into florets
2 courgettes (zucchini), sliced
250 g/ 8 oz asparagus spears, trimmed
125 g/ 4 oz mangetout (snow peas), trimmed
125 g/ 4 oz frozen peas • 30 g/ 1 oz/ 2 tbsp butter
3 tbsp vegetable stock • 5 tbsp double (heavy) cream
large pinch of freshly grated nutmeg • salt and pepper

1 Cook the pasta as described on page 11. Return the drained pasta to the saucepan, cover and keep warm.

2 To make the sauce, steam the broccoli, courgettes (zucchini), asparagus spears and mangetout (snow peas) over a pan of boiling, salted water until just beginning to soften. Remove from the heat and plunge into cold water to prevent further cooking. Drain and set aside. Cook the peas in boiling, salted water for 3 minutes, then drain. Refresh in cold water and drain again.

3 Put the butter and vegetable stock in a pan over a medium heat. Add all the vegetables except the asparagus spears and toss carefully with a wooden spoon, taking care not to break them up, until heated through. Stir in the cream, allow the sauce to just heat through and season well with salt, pepper and nutmeg.

4 Transfer the pasta to a warmed serving dish and stir in the chopped parsley. Spoon over the sauce, and sprinkle on the Parmesan. Arrange the asparagus spears on top. Serve hot.

Creamy Mushroom Vol-au-Vent

A simple mixture of creamy, tender mushrooms filling a crisp, rich pastry case.

SERVES 4

500 g / 1 lb 2 oz puff pastry, thawed if frozen
1 egg, beaten, for glazing

Filling:
30 g / 1 oz / 2 tbsp butter or margarine
750 g / 1½ lb mixed mushrooms such as open cup, field,
button, chestnut, shiitake, pied de mouton, sliced
6 tbsp dry white wine • 4 tbsp double (heavy) cream
2 tbsp chopped fresh chervil • salt and pepper
sprigs of fresh chervil, to garnish

1 Roll out the pastry on a lightly floured surface to a 20 cm/8 inch square. Using a sharp knife, mark a square 2.5 cm/1 inch from the pastry edge, cutting halfway through the pastry. Score the top in a diagonal pattern. Knock up the edges with a kitchen knife and put on a baking sheet (cookie sheet).

2 Brush the top with beaten egg, taking care not to let the egg run into the cut. Bake in a preheated oven, 220°C/425°F/Gas Mark 7, for 35 minutes. Cut out the central square. Discard the soft pastry inside the case, leaving the base intact. Bake the case and square for 10 minutes.

3 Meanwhile, make the filling. Melt the butter or margarine in a frying pan (skillet) and stir-fry the mushrooms over a high heat for 3 minutes. Add the wine and cook for 10 minutes, stirring occasionally, until the mushrooms have softened. Stir in the cream, chervil and seasoning. Pile into the pastry case. Top with the pastry square, garnish and serve.

Stir-Fried Winter Vegetables with Coriander (Cilantro)

Ordinary winter vegetables are given extraordinary treatment in this lively stir-fry, just the thing for perking up jaded palates.

SERVES 4

3 tbsp sesame oil • 30 g/1 oz/¼ cup blanched almonds
1 large carrot, cut into thin strips
1 large turnip, cut into thin strips
1 onion, sliced finely • 1 garlic clove, crushed
3 celery sticks, sliced finely
125 g/4 oz Brussels sprouts, trimmed and halved
125 g/4 oz cauliflower, broken into florets
125 g/4 oz/2 cups white cabbage, shredded
2 tsp sesame seeds • 1 tsp fresh root ginger, grated
½ tsp medium chilli powder
1 tbsp chopped fresh coriander (cilantro)
1 tbsp light soy sauce • salt and pepper
sprigs of fresh coriander (cilantro), to garnish

1 Heat the sesame oil in a wok or large frying pan (skillet). Stir-fry the almonds until lightly browned, then remove with a slotted spoon and drain on paper towels.

2 Add all the vegetables to the wok or frying pan (skillet), except for the cabbage. Stir-fry briskly for 3–4 minutes.

3 Add the cabbage, sesame seeds, ginger, chilli powder and salt and pepper and cook, stirring, for 2 minutes.

4 Add the chopped coriander (cilantro), soy sauce and almonds to the mixture, stirring them through gently. Serve hot, garnished with sprigs of fresh coriander (cilantro).

Vegetarian Pasta & Bean Casserole

A satisfying winter one-pot meal.

SERVES 6

250 g/8 oz/dried haricot beans, soaked overnight and drained
250 g/8 oz penne, or other short pasta shapes
6 tbsp olive oil • 900 ml/1½ pints/3½ cups vegetable stock
2 large onions, sliced • 2 garlic cloves, chopped • 2 bay leaves
1 tsp dried oregano • 1 tsp dried thyme • 5 tbsp red wine
2 tbsp tomato purée (paste) • 2 celery stalks, sliced
1 fennel bulb, sliced • 125 g/4 oz mushrooms, sliced
250 g/8 oz tomatoes, sliced • 1 tsp dark muscovado sugar
4 tbsp dry white breadcrumbs • salt and pepper

To serve:
salad leaves • crusty bread

1 Put the beans in a large pan, cover with water and bring to the boil. Boil the beans rapidly for 20 minutes, then drain them.

2 Cook the pasta for only 3 minutes in a large pan of boiling salted water, adding 1 tablespoon of the oil. Drain in a colander and set aside.

3 Put the beans in a large flameproof casserole, pour over the vegetable stock and stir in the remaining olive oil,

the onions, garlic, bay leaves, herbs, wine and tomato purée (paste). Bring to the boil, cover and cook in a preheated oven, 180°C/350°F/Gas Mark 4, for 2 hours.

4 Add the pasta, celery, fennel, mushrooms and tomatoes, and season. Stir in the sugar and sprinkle over the breadcrumbs. Cover the casserole and continue cooking for 1 hour. Serve hot, with salad leaves and plenty of crusty bread.

Vegetable Pasta Stir-Fry

For an extra-quick dish, prepare all the vegetables and cook the pasta in advance.

SERVES 4

*400 g/14 oz wholewheat pasta shells,
or other short pasta shapes
1 tbsp olive oil • 2 carrots, sliced thinly
125 g/4 oz baby sweetcorn cobs • 3 tbsp peanut oil
2.5 cm/1 inch piece of ginger root, sliced thinly
1 large onion, sliced thinly • 1 garlic clove, sliced thinly
3 celery stalks, sliced thinly
1 small red (bell) pepper, cored, deseeded and
sliced into matchsticks
1 small green (bell) pepper, cored, deseeded and
sliced into matchsticks
salt • steamed mangetout (snow peas), to serve*

Sauce:

*1 tsp cornflour (cornstarch) • 2 tbsp water
3 tbsp soy sauce • 3 tbsp dry sherry
1 tsp clear honey • few drops of hot pepper sauce (optional)*

1 Cook the pasta as described on page 11. Return to the pan, cover and keep warm.

2 Boil the carrots and sweetcorn in salted water for 2 minutes. Drain, plunge into cold water to prevent further cooking and drain.

3 Heat the peanut oil in a wok or large frying pan (skillet) over a medium heat and fry the ginger for 1 minute, to flavour the oil. Remove the ginger with a slotted spoon and discard.

4 Add the onion, garlic, celery and (bell) peppers to the oil and stir-fry for 2 minutes. Add the carrots and sweetcorn, and stir-fry for 2 minutes, then stir in the reserved pasta.

5 To make the sauce, put the cornflour (cornstarch) into a small bowl with the water and mix to a smooth paste. Stir in the soy sauce, sherry and honey. Pour the sauce into the wok, stir well and cook for 2 minutes, stirring occasionally. Taste the sauce and season with hot pepper sauce, if liked. Serve with a steamed green vegetable such as mangetout (snow peas).

Lentil Roast

The perfect dish for Sunday lunch.

SERVES 6

15 g/½ oz/1 tbsp butter or margarine, softened
2 tbsp dried wholemeal (whole wheat) breadcrumbs
250 g/8 oz/1 cup red lentils • 1 bay leaf
250 g/8 oz/2 cups mature (sharp) Cheddar, grated
1 leek, chopped finely
125 g/4 oz button mushrooms, chopped finely
90 g/3 oz/1½ cups fresh wholemeal (whole wheat)
breadcrumbs
2 tbsp chopped fresh parsley • 1 tbsp lemon juice
2 eggs, beaten lightly • salt and pepper
sprigs of flat-leaf parsley, to garnish
mixed roast vegetables, to serve

Vegetable stock
(makes 1.5 litres/2½ pints/6½ cups):
250 g/8 oz shallots • 1 large carrot, diced
1 celery stalk, chopped • ½ fennel bulb • 1 garlic clove
1 bay leaf • a few fresh parsley and tarragon sprigs
2 litres/3½ pints/9 cups water • pepper

1 To make the stock, put all the ingredients in a large saucepan and bring to the boil. Skim off surface scum and reduce to a simmer. Partially cover and cook for 45 minutes. Leave to cool. Strain the stock through a sieve (strainer) lined with clean muslin (cheesecloth) into a large jug or bowl. Discard the vegetables.

2 Base-line a 1 kg/2 lb loaf tin (pan) with baking parchment. Grease with the butter or margarine and sprinkle with the dried breadcrumbs.

3 Put the lentils, bay leaf and 500 ml/16 fl oz/ 2 cups of the stock in a saucepan. Bring to the boil, cover and simmer for 15–20

minutes until all the liquid is absorbed and the lentils have softened. Discard the bay leaf. Stir the cheese, leek, mushrooms, breadcrumbs and parsley into the lentils.

4 Bind the mixture together with the lemon juice and eggs. Season well and spoon into the prepared loaf tin (pan). Smooth the top and bake in a preheated oven, 190°C/375°F/Gas Mark 5, for 1 hour until golden.

5 Loosen the loaf with a palette knife (spatula) and turn on to a warmed serving plate. Garnish with sprigs of parsley and serve, sliced, with roast vegetables.

Mediterranean Spaghetti

Delicious Mediterranean vegetables, cooked in a rich tomato sauce, make an ideal topping for nutty wholewheat pasta.

SERVES 4

2 tbsp olive oil • 1 large red onion, chopped
2 garlic cloves, crushed • 1 tbsp lemon juice
4 baby aubergines (eggplant), quartered
600 ml/ 1 pint/ 2½ cups passata
2 tsp caster (superfine) sugar
2 tbsp tomato purée (paste)
400 g/ 14 oz can of artichoke hearts, drained and halved
125 g/ 4 oz/³⁄₄ cup pitted black olives
350 g/ 12 oz wholewheat dried spaghetti
salt and pepper • sprigs of fresh basil, to garnish
olive bread, to serve

1 Heat 1 tablespoon of the oil in a large frying pan (skillet) and gently fry the onion, garlic, lemon juice and aubergines (eggplant) for 4–5 minutes until lightly browned.

2 Pour in the passata, season with salt and pepper and add the sugar and tomato purée (paste). Bring to the boil, reduce the heat and simmer for 20 minutes.

3 Gently stir in the artichoke halves and olives and cook for 5 minutes.

4 Meanwhile, bring a large saucepan of lightly salted water to the boil and cook the spaghetti for 7–8 minutes until just tender. Drain well, toss in the remaining olive oil and season to taste.

5 Transfer the spaghetti to a warmed serving bowl and top with the vegetable sauce. Garnish with sprigs of basil and serve with olive bread.

Mexican Chilli Corn Pie

This bake of sweetcorn and kidney beans, is topped with crispy cheese cornbread.

SERVES 4

1 tbsp corn oil • 2 garlic cloves, crushed
1 red (bell) pepper, deseeded and diced
1 green (bell) pepper, deseeded and diced
1 celery stalk, diced • 1 tsp hot chilli powder
400 g/14 oz can of chopped tomatoes
325 g/11 oz can of sweetcorn, drained
200 g/7 oz can of kidney beans, drained and rinsed
2 tbsp chopped fresh coriander (cilantro) • salt and pepper
sprigs of fresh coriander (cilantro), to garnish
tomato and avocado salad, to serve

Topping:
125 g/4 oz/⅔ cup cornmeal
1 tbsp plain (all-purpose) flour • ½ tsp salt
2 tsp baking powder • 1 egg, beaten
90 ml/3½ fl oz/6 tbsp milk • 1 tbsp corn oil
125 g/4 oz/1¾ cups mature (sharp) Cheddar, grated

1 Heat the oil in a large frying pan (skillet) and gently fry the garlic, (bell) peppers and celery for 5–6 minutes until just softened.

2 Stir in the chilli powder, tomatoes, sweetcorn, beans and seasoning. Bring to the boil and simmer for 10 minutes. Stir in the coriander (cilantro) and spoon into an ovenproof dish.

3 To make the topping, mix together the cornmeal, flour, salt and baking powder. Make a well in the centre, add the egg, milk and oil and beat until a smooth batter is formed. Spoon over the (bell) pepper and sweetcorn mixture and sprinkle with the cheese. Bake in a preheated oven, 220°C/425°F/Gas Mark 7, for 25–30 minutes until golden and firm.

4 Garnish with coriander (cilantro) sprigs and serve immediately with a tomato and avocado salad.

Oriental-style Millet Pilau

Millet makes an interesting alternative to rice, which is the more traditional ingredient for a pilau.

SERVES 4

300 g/10 oz/1½ cups millet grains
1 tbsp vegetable oil
1 bunch spring onions (scallions), white and green parts, chopped
1 garlic clove, crushed • 1 tsp ginger root, grated
1 orange (bell) pepper, deseeded and diced
600 ml/1 pint/2½ cups water • 1 orange
125 g/4 oz/²/₃ cup chopped pitted dates
2 tsp sesame oil • 125 g/4 oz/1 cup roasted cashew nuts
2 tbsp pumpkin seeds • salt and pepper
oriental salad vegetables, to serve

1 Place the millet in a large saucepan and put over a medium heat for 4–5 minutes to toast, shaking the pan occasionally until the grains begin to crack and pop.

2 Heat the oil in another saucepan and gently fry the spring onions (scallions), garlic, ginger and (bell) pepper for 2–3 minutes until softened but not browned. Add the millet and pour in the water.

3 Using a vegetable peeler, pare the rind from the orange and add the rind to the pan. Squeeze the juice from the orange into the pan. Season well. Bring to the boil, reduce the heat, cover and cook gently for 20 minutes until all the liquid has been absorbed. Remove from the heat, stir in the dates and sesame oil and leave to stand for 10 minutes.

4 Discard the orange rind and stir in the cashew nuts. Pile into a serving dish, sprinkle with pumpkin seeds and serve with oriental salad vegetables.

Baked Aubergines (Eggplant) with Pasta

Pasta, tomatoes and Mozzarella make a tasty filling for baked aubergine (eggplant).

SERVES 4

250 g / 8 oz penne, or other short pasta shapes
4 tbsp olive oil, plus extra for brushing
2 aubergines (eggplant) • 1 large onion, chopped
2 garlic cloves, crushed
400 g / 14 oz can of chopped tomatoes • 2 tsp dried oregano
60 g / 2 oz Mozzarella, thinly sliced
30 g / 1 oz / ½ cup Parmesan, grated
2 tbsp dry breadcrumbs • salt and pepper
mixed salad leaves, to serve

1 Cook the pasta as described on page 11. Return to the pan, cover and keep warm.

2 Cut the aubergines (eggplant) in half lengthways. Score around the inside with a knife, then scoop out the flesh with a spoon, taking care not to pierce the skin. Brush the insides of the aubergine (eggplant) shells with olive oil. Chop the flesh and set it aside.

3 Heat the remaining oil in a frying pan (skillet) over a medium heat and fry the onion until it is translucent. Add the garlic and fry for 1 minute. Add the chopped aubergine (eggplant) and fry for 5 minutes, stirring frequently. Add the tomatoes and oregano, and season with salt and pepper. Bring to the boil and simmer for 10 minutes, or until the mixture is thick. Taste and adjust the seasoning if necessary. Remove from the heat and stir in the reserved pasta.

4 Brush a baking sheet (cookie sheet) with oil and arrange the aubergine (eggplant) shells in a single

layer. Divide half the tomato and pasta mixture between the four shells. Arrange the Mozzarella on top and cover with the remaining tomato and pasta mixture. Mix together the Parmesan and breadcrumbs, and sprinkle over the top, pressing it lightly into the mixture.

5 Bake in a preheated oven, 200°C/400°F/Gas Mark 6, for 25 minutes, until the topping is golden brown. Serve hot, with a mixed salad.

Spaghetti with Ricotta Cheese Sauce

This makes a quick and easy starter, ideal for the summer months.

SERVES 4

350 g/12 oz spaghetti • 1 tbsp olive oil
45 g/1½ oz/3 tbsp butter, cut into small pieces
2 tbsp chopped parsley

Sauce:

125 g/4 oz/1 cup freshly ground almonds
125 g/4 oz/½ cup Ricotta
large pinch of grated nutmeg
large pinch of ground cinnamon
150 ml/¼ pint/⅔ cup crème fraîche
2 tbsp olive oil
120 ml/4 fl oz/½ cup hot chicken stock
1 tbsp pine kernels
freshly ground black pepper
coriander (cilantro) leaves, to garnish

1 Cook the pasta as described on page 11. Return the drained pasta to the pan and toss with the butter and parsley. Cover the pan and keep warm.

2 To make the sauce, mix together the ground almonds, Ricotta, nutmeg, cinnamon and crème fraîche to make a thick paste. Gradually pour on the oil, stirring constantly until it is well blended. Gradually pour on the hot stock, stirring all the time, until the sauce is smooth.

3 Transfer the spaghetti to a warmed serving dish, pour on the sauce and toss well. Sprinkle each serving with pine kernels and garnish with coriander (cilantro) leaves. Serve warm.

Tagliatelle with Broccoli & Blue Cheese Sauce

This is a delicious combination of tagliatelle with Gorgonzola and Mascarpone cheese sauce.

SERVES 4

300 g / 10 oz tagliatelle tricolore (plain, spinach- and tomato-flavoured noodles)
250 g / 8 oz broccoli, broken into small florets
350g / 12 oz / 1½ cups Mascarpone cheese
125 g / 4 oz / 1 cup Gorgonzola cheese, chopped
1 tbsp chopped fresh oregano • 30 g / 1 oz / 2 tbsp butter
salt and pepper • sprigs of fresh oregano, to garnish
grated Parmesan cheese, to serve

1 Cook the tagliatelle in a pan of boiling, lightly salted water until just tender, or according to the instructions on the packet. The Italians call this *al dente*, which literally means 'to the tooth'.

2 Meanwhile, cook the broccoli florets in a small amount of lightly salted, boiling water. Avoid overcooking the broccoli, so that it retains its colour and texture.

3 Heat the Mascarpone and Gorgonzola cheeses together gently in a large saucepan until they have melted. Stir in the oregano and season to taste with salt and pepper.

4 Drain the pasta thoroughly. Return to the saucepan and add the butter, tossing the tagliatelle to coat. Drain the broccoli thoroughly and add to the pasta with the sauce, tossing gently to mix.

5 Divide the pasta between 4 warmed serving plates. Garnish with sprigs of fresh oregano and serve with grated Parmesan cheese.

Red Bean Stew & Dumplings

There's nothing better on a cold day than a hearty dish topped with dumplings. This recipe is quick and easy to prepare.

SERVES 4

1 tbsp vegetable oil • 1 red onion, sliced
2 celery stalks, chopped
900 ml/1½ pints/3½ cups vegetable stock
250 g/8 oz carrots, diced • 250 g/8 oz potatoes, diced
250 g/8 oz courgettes (zucchini), diced
4 tomatoes, peeled and chopped
125 g/4 oz/½ cup red lentils
400 g/14 oz can of kidney beans, rinsed and drained
1 tsp paprika • salt and pepper

Dumplings:
125 g/4 oz/1 cup plain (all-purpose) flour
½ tsp salt • 2 tsp baking powder
1 tsp paprika • 1 tsp dried mixed herbs
30 g/1 oz/2 tbsp vegetable suet • 7 tbsp water
sprigs of fresh flat-leaf parsley, to garnish

1 Heat the oil in a flameproof casserole or a large saucepan and gently fry the onion and celery for 3–4 minutes until just softened. Pour in the stock and stir in the carrots and potatoes. Bring to the boil, cover and cook for 5 minutes. Stir in the courgettes (zucchini), tomatoes, lentils, kidney beans, paprika and seasoning. Bring to the boil, cover and cook for 5 minutes.

2 Meanwhile, make the dumplings. Sift the flour, salt, baking powder and paprika into a bowl. Stir in the herbs and suet. Bind together with the water to form a soft

dough. Divide into 8 and roll into balls.

3 Uncover the stew, stir, then add the dumplings, pushing them slightly into the stew. Cover and reduce the heat to a simmer. Cook for 15 minutes until the dumplings have risen and are cooked through. Garnish with sprigs of flat-leaf parsley and serve hot.

Mediterranean Vegetable Tart

This rich tomato pastry base is topped with mouthwatering vegetables and cheese.

SERVES 6

*1 aubergine (eggplant), sliced • 2 tbsp salt
4 tbsp olive oil • 1 garlic clove, crushed
1 large yellow (bell) pepper, deseeded and sliced
300 ml/½ pint/1¼ cups ready-made tomato pasta sauce
125 g/4 oz/⅔ cup sun-dried tomatoes in oil,
drained and halved if necessary
175 g/6 oz Mozzarella, drained and sliced thinly*

Pastry:
*250 g/8 oz/2 cups plain (all-purpose) flour
pinch of celery salt • 125 g/4 oz/½ cup butter or margarine
2 tbsp tomato purée (paste) • 2–3 tbsp milk*

1 To make the pastry, sift the flour and celery salt into a bowl and rub in the butter or margarine until the mixture resembles fine breadcrumbs. Mix together the tomato purée (paste) and milk and stir into the mixture to form a firm dough. Knead gently on a lightly floured surface until smooth. Wrap and chill for 30 minutes.

2 Grease a 28 cm/11 inch loose-bottomed flan tin. Roll out the pastry on a lightly floured surface and use to line the tin. Trim and prick all over with a fork. Chill for 30 minutes.

3 Bake the pastry case in a preheated oven, 200°C/400°F/Gas Mark 6, for 20–25 minutes until cooked and lightly golden. Set aside. Increase the oven temperature to 230°C/450°F/Gas Mark 8.

4 Meanwhile, layer the aubergine (eggplant) in a

dish, sprinkling with the salt.
Leave for 30 minutes. Rinse
and pat dry. Heat 3
tablespoons of the oil in a
frying pan (skillet) and fry the
garlic, aubergine (eggplant)
and (bell) pepper for 5–6
minutes until just softened.
Drain on paper towels.

5 Spread the pastry case
with pasta sauce and
arrange the vegetables,
sun-dried tomatoes and
Mozzarella on top. Brush
with the remaining oil and
bake for 5 minutes until the
cheese is just melting.

Spinach Pancake Layer

Nutty-tasting buckwheat pancakes are combined with a cheesy spinach mixture and baked with a crispy topping.

SERVES 4

125 g/ 4 oz/ 1 cup buckwheat flour
1 egg, beaten • 1 tbsp walnut oil
300 ml/ ½ pint/ 1¼ cups milk • 2 tsp vegetable oil

Filling:

1 kg/ 2 lb young spinach leaves • 2 tbsp water
1 bunch spring onions (scallions), white and green parts, chopped
2 tsp walnut oil • 1 egg, beaten • 1 egg yolk
250 g/ 8 oz/ 1 cup cottage cheese • ½ tsp nutmeg, grated
30 g/ 1 oz/ ¼ cup mature (sharp) Cheddar, grated
30 g/ 1 oz/ ¼ cup walnut pieces • salt and pepper

1 Sift the flour into a bowl and add any husks that remain behind in the sieve (strainer). Make a well in the centre and add the egg and walnut oil. Gradually whisk in the milk to make a smooth batter. Leave to stand for 30 minutes.

2 To make the filling, wash the spinach and pack into a saucepan with the water. Cover tightly and cook on a high heat for 5–6 minutes until soft. Drain well and leave to cool. Gently fry the spring onions (scallions) in the walnut oil for 2–3 minutes until just soft. Drain on paper towels. Set aside.

3 Whisk the batter. Brush a small crêpe pan with oil, heat until hot and pour in enough batter to lightly cover the base. Cook for 1–2 minutes until set, turn and cook for 1 minute until golden. Turn on to a warmed plate. Repeat to make 8–10 pancakes, layering them with baking parchment.

4 Chop the spinach and dry with paper towels. Mix

with the spring onions (scallions), beaten egg, egg yolk, cottage cheese, nutmeg and seasoning.

5 Put a pancake on to a baking sheet (cookie sheet) lined with baking parchment, top with some of the spinach mixture and continue layering in this way, finishing with a pancake. Sprinkle with Cheddar cheese and bake in a preheated oven, 190°C/ 375°F/Gas Mark 5, for 20–25 minutes until firm and golden. Sprinkle with the walnuts and serve hot.

Pesto Rice with Garlic Bread

Two types of rice are combined with the richness of fresh pesto dressing.

SERVES 4

300 g/10 oz/1½ cups mixed long-grain and wild rice
fresh basil sprigs, to garnish • tomato and orange salad, to serve

Pesto dressing:

15 g/½ oz fresh basil • 125 g/4 oz/1 cup pine kernels (nuts)
2 garlic cloves, crushed • 6 tbsp olive oil
60 g/2 oz/¾ cup freshly grated Parmesan • salt and pepper

Garlic bread:

2 small granary or wholemeal (whole wheat) French bread sticks
90 g/3 oz/½ cup butter or margarine, softened
2 garlic cloves, crushed • 1 tsp dried mixed herbs

1 Place the rice in a saucepan and cover with water. Bring to the boil and cook according to the packet instructions. Drain well and keep warm.

2 Meanwhile, make the pesto dressing. Remove the basil leaves from the stalks and finely chop the leaves. Reserve 30 g/1 oz/ ¼ cup of the pine kernels (nuts) and finely chop the remainder. Mix with the chopped basil and the rest of the dressing ingredients. Alternatively, put all the ingredients in a food processor and blend for a few seconds until smooth. Set aside.

3 To make the garlic bread, slice the bread at 2.5 cm/ 1 inch intervals, taking care not to slice all the way through. Mix the butter or margarine with the garlic, herbs and seasoning. Spread thickly between each slice.

4 Wrap the bread in foil and bake in a preheated oven, 200°C/400°F/Gas Mark 6, for 10–15 minutes.

5 To serve, toast the reserved pine kernels (nuts) under a preheated medium grill (broiler) for 2–3 minutes until golden. Toss the pesto dressing into the hot rice and transfer to a warmed serving dish. Sprinkle with toasted pine kernels (nuts) and garnish with basil sprigs. Serve with the garlic bread and a tomato and orange salad.

Spicy Coconut Rice with Green Lentils

This recipe will serve 2 people as a main course or 4 as an accompaniment.

SERVES 2–4

90 g/3 oz/⅓ cup green lentils
250 g/8 oz/generous 1 cup long-grain rice
2 tbsp vegetable oil • 1 onion, sliced
2 garlic cloves, crushed • 3 curry leaves
1 stalk lemon grass, chopped (if unavailable,
use rind of ½ lemon, grated)
1 green chilli, deseeded and chopped • ½ tsp cumin seeds
1½ tsp salt • 90 g/3 oz/⅓ cup creamed coconut
600 ml/1 pint/2½ cups hot water
2 tbsp chopped fresh coriander (cilantro)

To garnish:
shredded radishes • shredded cucumber

1 Wash the lentils and place in a saucepan. Cover with cold water, bring to the boil and boil rapidly for 10 minutes. Wash the rice thoroughly and drain well.

2 Heat the oil in a large saucepan with a tight-fitting lid and fry the onion for 3–4 minutes. Add the garlic, curry leaves, lemon grass, chilli, cumin seeds and salt, and stir well.

3 Drain the lentils and rinse. Add to the onion and spices with the rice and mix well. Add the creamed coconut to the hot water and stir until dissolved. Stir into the rice mixture and bring to the boil. Turn down the heat to low, put the lid on tightly and leave to cook undisturbed for 15 minutes.

4 Without removing the lid, remove the pan from the heat and leave to rest for 10

minutes to allow the rice and
lentils to finish cooking in
their own steam. Stir in the
coriander (cilantro) and

remove the curry leaves.
Serve garnished with
shredded radishes
and cucumber.

(Bell) Peppers with Rosemary Baste

The flavour of grilled (broiled) or roasted (bell) peppers is very different from when they are eaten raw.

SERVES 4

4 tbsp olive oil
finely grated rind of 1 lemon
4 tbsp lemon juice
1 tbsp balsamic vinegar
1 tbsp crushed fresh rosemary, or 1 tsp dried rosemary
2 red (bell) peppers, halved, cored and deseeded
2 yellow (bell) peppers, halved, cored and deseeded
2 tbsp pine kernels (nuts)
salt and pepper
sprigs of fresh rosemary, to garnish

1 Mix together the olive oil, lemon rind, lemon juice, vinegar and rosemary. Season with salt and pepper.

2 Place the (bell) peppers, skin-side uppermost, on the rack of a grill (broiler) pan, lined with foil. Brush the lemon juice mixture over them.

3 Cook the (bell) peppers until the skin just begins to char, basting frequently with the lemon juice mixture. Remove from the heat, cover with foil to trap the steam and leave for 5 minutes.

4 Meanwhile, scatter the pine kernels (nuts) on to the grill (broiler) rack and toast them lightly.

5 Peel the (bell) peppers, slice them into strips and place them in a warmed serving dish. Sprinkle with the pine kernels and drizzle any remaining lemon juice mixture over them. Garnish with sprigs of fresh rosemary and serve at once.

Roast Leeks

Use a good-quality French or Italian olive oil for this deliciously simple yet sophisticated vegetable accompaniment.

SERVES 4–6

4 leeks
3 tbsp olive oil
2 tsp balsamic vinegar
sea salt and pepper

1 Halve the leeks lengthways, so that the leek is held together by the root. Rinse the leeks thoroughly to remove any dirt or grit and dry well.

2 Brush each leek liberally with the olive oil.

3 Cook the leeks over a hot barbecue for 6–7 minutes, turning once.

4 Remove the leeks from the barbecue and brush with the balsamic vinegar.

5 Sprinkle with sea salt and pepper and serve hot or warm.

Desserts

Fruit features prominently in these sumptuous desserts, reflecting the exotic fruits widely available today. There are even a selection of desserts for your barbecue. In addition, the Italian desserts in this chapter, such as Tiramisu, are sure to provide a deliciously wicked end to a meal!

Green Fruit Salad with Mint & Lemon Syrup

This delightful fresh fruit salad is the perfect finale for a summer meal. It has a lovely light syrup made with fresh mint and honey.

SERVES 4

*1 small Charentais or honeydew melon
2 green apples • 2 kiwi fruit
125 g/4 oz/1 cup seedless white (green) grapes
sprigs of fresh mint to decorate*

Syrup:

*1 lemon • 150 ml/¼ pint/⅔ cup white wine
150 ml/¼ pint/⅔ cup water
4 tbsp clear honey • few sprigs of fresh mint*

1 To make the syrup, pare the rind from the lemon using a potato peeler.

2 Put the lemon rind into a saucepan with the wine, water and honey. Heat and simmer gently for 10 minutes. Remove from the heat. Add the sprigs of mint and leave to cool.

3 Slice the melon in half and scoop out the seeds. Use a melon baller or a teaspoon to make melon balls.

4 Core and chop the apples. Peel and slice the kiwi fruit.

5 Strain the cooled syrup into a serving bowl, removing and reserving the lemon rind and discarding the mint sprigs. Add the apple, grapes, kiwi and melon. Stir through gently to mix.

6 Serve, decorated with sprigs of fresh mint and some of the reserved lemon rind.

Banana & Marshmallow Melts with Butterscotch Sauce

This delicious dessert will go down a treat with everyone. Bananas and marshmallows taste fantastic with the butterscotch sauce.

SERVES 4

4 bananas
4 tbsp lemon juice
250 g/ 8 oz packet of marshmallows

Butterscotch sauce:
125 g/ 4 oz/ ½ cup butter
125 g/ 4 oz/ ⅓ cup light muscovado sugar
125 g/ 4 oz/ ⅓ cup golden (light corn) syrup
4 tbsp hot water

1 Soak 4 wooden skewers in hand-hot water for 30 minutes. Slice the bananas into large chunks and dip them into the lemon juice to prevent them going brown. Thread 2 marshmallows and 1 piece of banana alternately on to each skewer.

2 To make the sauce, melt the butter, sugar and syrup together in a small saucepan. Add the hot water, stirring until blended and smooth. Do not boil or the mixture will thicken to toffee. Keep the sauce warm at the edge of the barbecue, stirring from time to time.

3 Sear the kebabs over the hot barbecue for 30–40 seconds, turning constantly, so that the marshmallows just begin to brown and melt. Serve the kebabs with some of the butterscotch sauce spooned over, or use as a dipping sauce.

Tiramisu

A favourite Italian dessert flavoured with coffee and Amaretto. You could substitute the Amaretto with brandy or Marsala.

SERVES 4–6

20–24 sponge fingers (lady-fingers), about 150 g/5 oz
2 tbsp cold black coffee • 2 tbsp coffee essence
2 tbsp Amaretto • 4 egg yolks
90 g/3 oz/½ cup caster (superfine) sugar
few drops of vanilla essence • grated rind of ½ lemon
350 g/12 oz Mascarpone cheese (Italian full-fat cream cheese)
2 tsp lemon juice
250 ml/8 fl oz/1 cup double (heavy) cream
1 tbsp milk
30 g/1 oz/⅓ cup flaked (slivered) almonds, lightly toasted
2 tbsp cocoa powder • 1 tbsp icing (confectioners') sugar

1 Arrange almost half the sponge fingers (lady-fingers) in the base of a glass bowl or serving dish. Combine the black coffee, coffee essence and Amaretto and pour just over half of the mixture over the fingers.

2 Put the egg yolks into a heatproof bowl with the sugar, vanilla essence and lemon rind. Stand over a saucepan of gently simmering water and whisk until very thick and creamy and the whisk leaves a very heavy trail when lifted from the bowl.

3 Put the Mascarpone cheese in a bowl with the lemon juice and beat until smooth. Combine the egg and Mascarpone cheese mixtures and when evenly blended pour half over the sponge fingers (lady-fingers) and spread out evenly.

4 Add another layer of fingers, sprinkle with the remaining coffee and Amaretto mixture and then cover with the rest of the cheese mixture. Chill for at least 2 hours, or overnight.

5 To serve, whip the cream and milk together until stiff and spread or pipe over the dessert. Sprinkle with the flaked (slivered) almonds and then sift an even layer of cocoa powder so the top is covered. Finally, sift a light layer of icing (confectioners') sugar over the cocoa.

Ricotta Ice Cream

Ice cream is a traditional Italian dish, and the numerous flavours available are usually sold in a cone. It is also served sliced.

SERVES 4–6

30 g/ 1 oz/ ¼ cup pistachio nuts
30 g/ 1 oz/ ¼ cup walnuts or pecan nuts
30 g/ 1 oz/ ¼ cup chopped hazelnuts, toasted
grated rind of 1 orange • grated rind of 1 lemon
30 g/ 1 oz/ 2 tbsp crystallized or stem ginger
30 g/ 1 oz/ 2 tbsp glacé (candied) cherries
30 g/ 1 oz/ ¼ cup dried apricots
30 g/ 1 oz/ 3 tbsp raisins
500 g/ 1 lb 2 oz Ricotta
2 tbsp Maraschino, Amaretto or brandy
1 tsp vanilla essence • 4 egg yolks
125 g/ 4 oz/ ⅔ cup caster (superfine) sugar

To decorate:
whipped cream
a few glacé cherries, pistachio nuts or mint leaves

1 Roughly chop the pistachio nuts and walnuts and mix with the toasted hazelnuts, orange and lemon rinds. Finely chop the ginger, cherries, apricots and raisins, and add to the bowl. Stir the Ricotta evenly through the fruit mixture, then beat in the liqueur and vanilla essence.

2 Put the egg yolks and sugar in a bowl and whisk hard until very thick and creamy – they may be whisked over a pan of gently simmering water to speed up the process. Leave to cool if necessary. Carefully fold the Ricotta mixture evenly through the beaten eggs and sugar until smooth.

3 Line a 18 × 12 cm/ 7 × 5 inch loaf tin (pan) with a double layer of cling

film (plastic wrap) or baking parchment. Pour in the Ricotta mixture, level the top, cover with more cling film (plastic wrap) or baking parchment and chill in the freezer until firm – at least overnight.

4 To serve, remove the ice-cream from the tin (pan) and peel off the cling film or parchment. Place on a serving dish and decorate with whipped cream, glacé (candied) cherries, pistachio nuts or mint leaves.

Blackberry, Apple & Fresh Fig Compote with Honey Yogurt

Elderflower cordial is used in the syrup for this refreshing fruit compote, giving it a delightfully summery flavour.

SERVES 4

1 lemon
60 g/2 oz/¼ cup caster (superfine) sugar
4 tbsp elderflower cordial
300 ml/½ pint/1¼ cups water
4 dessert (eating) apples
250 g/8 oz/2 cups blackberries
2 fresh figs

Honey yogurt:
150 ml/5 fl oz/⅔ cup thick, creamy natural yogurt
2 tbsp clear honey

1 Pare the rind from the lemon using a potato peeler. Squeeze the juice. Put the lemon rind and juice into a saucepan with the sugar, elderflower cordial and water. Heat gently and simmer, uncovered, for 10 minutes.

2 Peel, core and slice the apples, and add them to the saucepan. Simmer gently for 4–5 minutes until just tender. Leave to cool.

3 Transfer the apples and syrup to a serving bowl and add the blackberries. Slice the figs and add to the bowl. Toss gently to mix. Cover and chill until ready to serve.

4 Spoon the yogurt into a small serving bowl and drizzle the honey over the top. Cover and chill, then serve with the fruit salad.

Tropical Fruit Kebabs

Sear some chunks of exotic tropical fruits over the barbecue and serve with this amazing chocolate dip.

SERVES 4

4 wooden skewers

Chocolate dip:

125 g / 4 oz / 4 squares plain (dark) chocolate, broken into pieces
2 tbsp golden (light corn) syrup
1 tbsp cocoa powder • 1 tbsp cornflour (cornstarch)
200 ml / 7 fl oz / generous ³⁄₄ cup milk

Kebabs:

1 mango • 1 paw-paw (papaya) • 2 kiwi fruit
½ small pineapple • 1 large banana
2 tbsp lemon juice • 150 ml / ¼ pint / ²⁄₃ cup white rum

1 Soak 4 wooden skewers in hand-hot water for 30 minutes.

2 Put all the ingredients for the chocolate dip into a saucepan. Heat, stirring constantly, until thickened and smooth. Keep warm at the edge of the barbecue.

3 Slice the mango on each side of its large, flat stone (pit). Cut the flesh into chunks, removing the peel. Halve, deseed and peel the paw-paw (papaya) and cut it into chunks. Peel the kiwi fruit and slice into chunks. Peel and cut the pineapple into chunks. Peel and slice the banana and dip the pieces in the lemon juice.

4 Thread the pieces of fruit alternately on to the wooden skewers. Place them in a shallow dish and pour over the rum. Leave to soak up the flavour of the rum until ready to barbecue, at least 30 minutes.

5 Cook the kebabs over the hot barbecue, turning

frequently, until seared, about 2 minutes.

6 Serve, accompanied by the hot chocolate dip.

Zabaglione

**Serve this light dessert warm or chilled,
accompanied by sponge fingers
(lady-fingers) or amaretti biscuits,
and soft fruits.**

SERVES 4

6 egg yolks
90 g/3 oz/½ cup caster (superfine) sugar
6 tbsp Marsala
strawberries or raspberries (optional)
amaretti biscuits or sponge fingers (lady-fingers) (optional)

1 Put the egg yolks into a heatproof bowl and whisk until a pale yellow colour, using a rotary, balloon or electric whisk.

2 Whisk in the caster (superfine) sugar, followed by the Marsala, continuing to whisk all the time.

3 Stand the bowl over a saucepan of very gently simmering water, or transfer to the top of a double boiler, and continue to whisk until the mixture thickens sufficiently to form soft peaks. On no account allow the water to boil or the zabaglione will over-cook and turn into scrambled eggs. Scrape around the sides of the bowl from time to time while whisking. As soon as the mixture is really thick and foamy, remove from the heat and continue to whisk for a couple of minutes longer.

4 Pour immediately into stemmed glasses and serve warm; or leave until cold and serve chilled.

5 Fruits such as strawberries or raspberries, or crumbled sponge fingers (lady-fingers) or amaretti biscuits may be placed in the base of the glasses before adding the zabaglione.

Panforte di Siena

This famous Tuscan honey and nut cake is a Christmas speciality. In Italy it is sold in pretty boxes, and served in very thin slices.

SERVES 12

125 g/ 4 oz/ ³⁄₄ cup split whole almonds
125 g/ 4 oz/ 1 cup hazelnuts
90 g/ 3 oz/ ½ cup cut mixed peel
60 g/ 2 oz/ ⅓ cup no-soak dried apricots
60 g/ 2 oz glacé or crystallized pineapple
grated rind of 1 large orange
60 g/ 2 oz/ ⅔ cup plain (all-purpose) flour
2 tbsp cocoa powder • 2 tsp ground cinnamon
125 g/ 4 oz/ ½ cup caster (superfine) sugar
175 g/ 6 oz/ ³⁄₄ cup honey
icing (confectioners') sugar, for dredging

1 Toast the almonds under the grill (broiler) until lightly browned and place in a bowl. Toast the hazelnuts until the skins split. Place on a dry tea towel (dish cloth) and rub off the skins. Roughly chop the hazelnuts and add to the almonds with the mixed peel. Chop the apricots and pineapple finely, add to the nuts with the orange rind and mix well.

2 Sift the flour with the cocoa and cinnamon, add to the nut mixture and mix evenly.

3 Line a round 20 cm/ 8 inch cake tin or deep loose-based flan tin with baking parchment.

4 Put the sugar and honey into a saucepan and heat until the sugar dissolves, then boil gently for about 5 minutes or until the mixture thickens and begins to turn a deeper shade of brown. Quickly add to the nut mixture and mix evenly. Turn into the prepared tin and level the top using the back of a damp spoon.

5 Cook in a preheated oven, 150°C/300°F/Gas Mark 2, for 1 hour. Remove from the oven and leave in the tin until cold. Remove from the tin and peel off the baking parchment. Before serving, dredge the cake with sifted icing (confectioners') sugar. Serve in thin slices.

Index

Index compiled by Hilary Bird